allergy-friendly food for families

allergy-friendly food for families

120 GLUTEN-FREE, DAIRY-FREE, NUT-FREE, EGG-FREE, AND SOY-FREE RECIPES EVERYONE WILL LOVE

EDITORS OF kiwi MAGAZINE

FOREWORD BY ROBYN O'BRIEN

**Andrews McMeel
Publishing, LLC**
Kansas City • Sydney • London

Dedicated to the kiwi readers who handle their children's food challenges with such patience, diligence, and love. You inspire us every day to live healthy, happy, delicious lives.

Andrews McMeel Publishing, LLC
an Andrews McMeel Universal company
1130 Walnut Street, Kansas City, Missouri 64106

www.andrewsmcmeel.com

12 13 14 15 16 TEN 10 9 8 7 6 5 4 3 2 1

ISBN: 978-1-4494-0976-0

Library of Congress Control Number: 2011932640

www.kiwimagonline.com

Design: Theresa Izzillo

Book Composition: Diane Marsh

Food Photography: Ghazalle Badiozamani
ii, 4, 11, 18, 29, 32, 42, 51, 54, 59, 62, 69, 77, 85, 90, 95, 100, 112, 118, 123, 128, 133, 136, 147, 150, 159, 164, 169, 183, 188, 195, 200, 207

Food Stylist: Toni Brogan

Prop Stylist: Laura Hart

Lifestyle Photography: Alexandra Grablewski
viii, xvi, 36, 72, 108, 142, 174, 214

Stylist: Nancy Smith

Personal Stylist: Noelle Marinelli

The information contained in this book is not intended to replace regular visits with your physician or to diagnose deficiencies in your diet. Before altering your diet you should always check with your physician about your specific needs. The information and recipes in this book are intended to benefit people with allergies as part of a healthy diet in conjunction with a doctor's supervision. While every effort was made to assure that the information and recipes are nutritionally sound and balanced for those with allergies, the author and publisher are not liable for any adverse effects you may experience.

contents

Acknowledgments vi

Foreword by Robyn O'Brien vii

Introduction: Welcome to the "-Free" Life ix

Ask the Experts xiii

BREAKFAST .1

LUNCH 37

DINNER 73

DESSERT 109

SNACKS 143

PARTIES 175

Building a Natural, Allergy-Free Pantry 213

Metric Conversions and Equivalents 222

Recipe Index by Allergen 224

Index 230

acknowledgments

This cookbook could not have been created without the creativity, brains, and long hours over the stove of KIWI staff recipe developer Marygrace Taylor. Most of the recipes in this book came straight from her kitchen in Austin, Texas, and the rest of the KIWI family thanks her for her good nature and delicious food.

Several other recipe developers were invaluable in rounding out the recipes in this book: Stephanie Stiavetti, Keri Fisher, Jeanne Ambrose, Andrea Lynn, Charmian Christie, Christina Stanley-Salerno, and Diana Burrell. Thank you for bringing us your fresh ideas. Mary Talalay and Debbie Koenig provided important research and writing, and registered dietitians Amanda Buthmann and Julie McGinnis gave us valuable feedback on our recipes.

For the beautiful photography and styling, we are grateful to Ghazalle Badiozamani, Laura Hart, Toni Brogan, Alexandra Grablewski, Nancy Smith, and Noelle Marinelli. Without your talents, we wouldn't have been able to showcase how delicious allergy-friendly food can be.

Theresa Izzillo's design work brought everything together, and KIWI staffers Sarah Smith, Maxine Wolf, Frank Giacobbe, Annie Douglass, and Amy Beal all contributed their expertise. KIWI would especially like to thank our editor at Andrews McMeel, Jean Lucas, for helping us make our first book a reality.

Thanks to the organic-clothing companies that provided the adorable outfits the kids and parents in the photos are wearing, including Funny Hunny Bunny; Winter Water Factory; and Green Cotton, Duns Sweden + Roda Hund, Maxomorra, and Sture Lisa (all for Vyssan Lull).

This cookbook has been a true team effort; and we also thank all the other friends, family members, colleagues, and business partners who offered their support and encouragement.

foreword

The landscape of childhood has changed. In the last several years, we have seen jaw-dropping increases in the rates of allergies, autism, ADHD, and asthma, earning these conditions the nickname "the 4 A's" and our children the title "Generation Rx." Today, it is estimated that food allergies affect at least one out of seventeen kids under the age of three, with a study showing a doubling of peanut allergy from 1997 to 2002. And according to an October 2008 study by the Centers for Disease Control and Prevention, there has been a 265 percent increase in the rate of hospitalizations related to food allergic reactions.

And as we work to protect our food allergic families from the hidden dangers that foods can present, a growing number of us are finding our ways into the kitchen in an effort to prepare foods that are both safe and nutritious for our families. For some, like me, this may be an intimidating task. Because until a few years ago, I couldn't cook. But when my youngest child had an allergic reaction one morning over breakfast, which in all candor included blue yogurt, frozen waffles, and scrambled eggs, life changed. And like so many of you, I was thrown onto this new landscape of childhood and into the kitchen in an effort to manage these food allergies.

And in learning to cook, I realized that we can take the fear out of food and make it fun.

To be honest, I've burnt everything from pancakes to noodles, but I've also learned that the most important ingredient in any recipe is love. So I invite you to pull up a chair, flip through *Allergy-Friendly Food for Families*, and soak in the love and wholesome goodness that are tucked into these pages. *Allergy-Friendly Food for Families* is an invaluable resource for those interested in protecting the health of their families.

And remember, while none of us can do everything, all of us can do something. So pick a recipe and get started, because with inspiration, practical suggestions, heartfelt instructions, and real-world solutions, *Allergy-Friendly Food for Families* is both a sound investment in the health of your family and a resource that will pay dividends for a lifetime.

~Robyn O'Brien
AUTHOR OF *THE UNHEALTHY TRUTH*,
FOUNDER OF THE ALLERGYKIDS FOUNDATION

introduction

welcome to the "-free" life

FOOD AND FAMILY go together like bacon and eggs, bread and butter, milk and cookies—right? Well, yes, they're great combos—for some people. But when you don't eat eggs and your kids can't stomach milk, it can start to feel like food is out to get your family, not bring it together.

In the millions of homes where someone—mom, dad, kid, or baby—has a food allergy or other reason to eliminate certain ingredients, sharing a meal can be tricky. All families have to cope with busy schedules, finicky taste buds, and how to stay healthy. But when whole categories of food are off-limits, you're at a whole new level of parenting. At KIWI, we're all about raising healthy, happy families. We hear from worried moms and dads with questions like: What can we serve when one kid's allergic to wheat and Dad can't eat dairy? Do we have to cook three different meals? Where are we going to shop? Will we ever have brunch again?

The answers to these questions may all be different, but one thing is certain: You will have brunch again. And it's going to be delicious.

UNDERSTANDING FOOD ALLERGIES

Despite all of the education and awareness about food allergies, myths persist that food allergies are just the signs of a picky eater or an overprotective parent. Explaining this to the mom handing out her "harmless" cupcakes can get exhausting, especially when what you need to do—pronto—is find out exactly what ingredients she used and whether there were nuts anywhere near the mixing bowl.

A food allergy causes a person's immune system to overreact to the proteins contained in otherwise harmless food. Common symptoms of a food allergic reaction can include stomachache, cramps, diarrhea, vomiting, itchy or tingly mouth, or throat itching or tightening. Everyone has a different threshold for the amount of unsafe food he can ingest, and reacting mildly today doesn't predict how your body will react tomorrow.

Sometimes people experience food allergy–like symptoms that actually indicate a food intolerance or food sensitivity. For instance, lactose intolerance is not an allergy, because it stems from the body's difficulty digesting the sugars in milk—it's not a reaction from the body's immune system the way a dairy allergy is. The only way to know for sure exactly what is happening is to be tested by a certified allergist.

KEEPING YOUR FAMILY SAFE

Once you've determined that someone in your family has a food allergy, you'll face a new challenge: Adjusting your shopping list so that you're 100 percent sure that nothing you're buying poses a risk.

Until a few years ago, having a child with a food allergy required the sleuthing abilities of Sherlock Holmes—food labels were filled with ingredient names that didn't mean much to most people. So unless a parent learned, for example, that casein is a milk derivative, he might have unknowingly endangered his child. That changed with the Food Allergen Labeling and Consumer Protection Act (FALCPA), which requires all food manufactured after January 1, 2006, to be clearly labeled when it contains any of eight major allergens: milk, eggs, fish, shellfish, tree nuts, peanuts, wheat, and soybeans. Here's how it works:

- Labels must identify in plain English any of those allergens, or foods that contain a protein derived from them. So flour must use the word "wheat" if it's milled from that grain, and when lecithin comes from soy, it'll say so.

- This labeling can happen in one of two ways. The allergen may appear within the ingredients list—for example, "flour (wheat)"—or in a statement following the list—"Contains wheat." Manufacturers decide which option to use, and they aren't required to do both, so you must read the entire label.

While FALCPA has done an awful lot to make it easier to live with food allergies, some holes remain in the regulations, which the FDA is working to address:

- Cross-contact, which occurs when a trace amount of an allergenic food is unintentionally added during production, is not covered by FALCPA. Many manufacturers do include a statement on their labels, something like "Produced in a plant that processes peanuts," but that's currently voluntary. If it's not mentioned, your best chance of reassurance is to call the manufacturer, however impractical that may sound. Accidental exposure can happen, so if your child is extremely sensitive you should always be prepared.

- Wheat is covered under FALCPA, but gluten is not. For several years the FDA has been examining various possibilities for gluten-free labeling, but currently it, too, is voluntary. The only way to avoid gluten is to read labels extremely carefully, and to familiarize yourself with less-obvious sources—which includes such things as bulgur, seitan, and most malt products. One excellent list is at www.celiacdisease.net/gluten-free-diet.

As you read through the recipes in *Allergy-Friendly Food for Families,* you might find ingredients you didn't know much about before, like almond flour or xanthan gum. Be sure to flip to the Building a Natural, Allergy-Free Pantry section at the end of the book to bone up on allergy-friendly ingredients, and learn about companies that make safe products.

Once you've bought and safely used a product, you may assume you're good to go—but manufacturers tweak their recipes all the time, so something that was allergen-free last week may not be today. Remember: *Always read the labels. Every time.*

LIVING THE "-FREE" LIFE
Handling allergies and food issues can be a challenge, but at KIWI, we don't think of it as a *problem*. Living "-free" is a great, healthy, fulfilling way to raise a family. When you cut out certain foods and become a family that eats gluten-free, soy-free, or whatever the case, you're also opening yourselves up to a whole new world of healthy, tasty options.

We encourage people to choose organic when they can—for the health of their families and the planet. It's especially important for families with food allergies and intolerances to know exactly what they're eating, so organic just makes sense: You're avoiding chemicals, pesticides, and unknown additives. We also never recommend artificial ingredients, including dyes and flavors. Some of these (like

KIWI recommends ORGANIC ingredients

Red 40 and Yellow 5) have been linked to behavioral problems in kids; the effects of some other chemicals in people's bodies haven't been researched enough yet, and we believe in the precautionary principle, especially for those with allergies. If you aren't sure whether something might cause harm, just avoid it and choose what you know to be safe. All of the recipes in this book call for wholesome ingredients that you can feel good about giving your family. When you shop for them, look for the USDA Organic seal, read labels, and enjoy the delicious whole foods that are safe for you.

People with allergies aren't the only ones living the "-free" life. Many parents are finding that a gluten-free and casein-free diet (GFCF) is helpful for their children with autism and ADHD. Advocates of the GFCF diet believe it keeps improperly digested proteins from interfering with the brain; without the problem proteins, kids (and adults) have better concentration and social skills. Eliminating gluten and casein can be a perfectly safe option to try, and if you are giving it a shot, you will find plenty of recipes in this book to support you.

Whatever reason your family has for limiting or eliminating foods, *Allergy-Friendly Food for Families* has dozens of recipes that are safe, simple to make, and tasty for everyone in the family. No more complaints that someone misses his favorite food because his brother can't eat it, no more short-order cooking for Mom or Dad, and no more feeling left out because everyone else gets to have pie. Everybody can have a slice of Coconut No-Cream Pie—but after, of course, they eat their dairy-free Mac-n-Cheeze or gluten-free Pizza Pockets. The best thing about these recipes is that kids love the way dishes like Veggie Bite Soup and Butternut Blondies taste, and parents can feel just as good about the ingredients in them (like quinoa and flaxseed).

We've focused on the five most common food allergens—gluten, dairy, nuts, eggs, and soy— and each recipe is clearly marked with colorful tabs that indicate which allergens the recipe is free of (see left). If the Gluten-Free, Soy-Free, or any other tab also says "option," then there's an easy substitution, spelled out right in the recipe, that'll make the recipe safe for that allergen. Get to know which colors you need the most (your child is allergic to nuts? Keep an eye out for the red tabs), and you'll be able to flip through the book to find new recipes quickly. We've organized the book by type of meal (breakfast, lunch, dinner), but we were sure to include entire chapters on staples of kids' lives that can be especially difficult for parents when you're dealing with an allergy: snacks, parties, and desserts. Meals are crucial—but to kids, so are parties.

And though you may be looking for what's *excluded*, we've made sure we *included* good-for-you, tasty ingredients, too. One key ingredient in every single recipe? Yumminess. Giving you a doable alternative to "regular" food isn't enough: It has to make you forget the other stuff altogether.

We also know that kids are more open to trying new foods when they can get involved in the kitchen—and that including them can be a lot of goofy, sometimes messy, fun—so look for Cooking with Kids instructions throughout. These step-by-step lessons might even teach Mom and Dad a few techniques!

You're sure to discover some new favorites in *Allergy-Friendly Food for Families*. And we hope you find that allergy-friendly food and your family are a great combo . . . kind of like dairy-free milk and gluten-free cookies.

ask the experts

HOW CAN I SPOT A FOOD ALLERGY?

Food allergies can affect children as young as infants but can develop at any age. The most common symptoms of a food-allergic reaction are stomachache, cramps, diarrhea, vomiting, itchy or tingly mouth, or throat itching or tightening. To describe an allergic reaction in progress, your young child might say that her mouth or throat feels bumpy, her tongue feels bigger, or food tastes too spicy. Infants and children can also develop eczema in response to a food.

Symptoms can occur several minutes to two hours after eating an allergen, and life-threatening reactions may occur and then worsen over a period of several hours, according to the Food Allergy and Anaphylaxis Network (FAAN).

WHAT SHOULD I DO IF I SUSPECT MY CHILD HAS A FOOD ALLERGY?

If your child is experiencing difficulty breathing, call 911 immediately. Difficulty breathing is a sign of anaphylaxis, which is a serious allergic reaction that comes on quickly and can be fatal. Tree nuts and peanuts are the leading causes of anaphylaxis, according to the National Institutes of Health (NIH).

If your child is having a mild reaction such as itching or tingling or stomach discomfort, you should note the type, preparation, and amount of the food eaten and follow up with a call to your physician. Your physician will refer you to a board-certified allergist for consultation and testing.

CAN A CHILD GROW OUT OF A FOOD ALLERGY?

FAAN estimates that about 85 percent of children who are allergic to milk or eggs will outgrow their food allergy, and just about all children who are allergic to soy or wheat will outgrow their allergy. (Note that celiac disease is not the same as an allergy: It is an autoimmune disease, and children who have it will not outgrow their intolerance to gluten.) Most children outgrow their food allergies to milk, egg, soy, and wheat by the time they are ten years old, and often before five years of age. Peanut, tree nut, fish, or shellfish allergies are more likely to last a lifetime. You can have your child retested as he grows.

HOW MUCH OF A FOOD ALLERGEN DOES IT TAKE TO CAUSE A REACTION?

Even trace amounts can cause a reaction. For example, perhaps you're making a few batches of cookies, simply using the same spoon to mix a "nut-free" batch and one with nuts. Using the same spoon or baking pan can contaminate all of the cookies and cause a severe reaction if an allergic person eats the "nut-free" cookie. For unknown reasons, some foods contain a protein that seems to more readily cause an allergic reaction, and/or a more severe reaction. Peanut protein and tree nut protein are examples of food protein that are more likely to cause a severe food allergy episode than something like an egg protein.

WILL EATING A LITTLE BIT OF A FOOD HELP A PERSON DEVELOP A RESISTANCE TO HIS ALLERGY?

No, it's not safe to try to help your child overcome a food allergy by giving him a problem food in small doses. It's better to avoid the food entirely and have your child retested by an allergy specialist as he gets older. Also, it's important to focus your energy on avoiding the specific food your child is allergic to: Other foods, even though they may seem similar, may not cause a reaction. For example, if a person is allergic to peanuts, they are not necessarily allergic to tree nuts such as almonds or pecans. Some specialists are exploring how food trials can help desensitize kids to allergens by exposing them to tiny amounts of the food in question, but the research is still experimental.

HOW CAN PARENTS MAKE SURE THEIR ALLERGIC KID STILL GETS THE NUTRIENTS HE NEEDS?

Families should try to keep in mind all the foods that kids *can* safely eat and enjoy. If your child is allergic to milk, for instance, he can still eat all fruits and vegetables, grains, meat, fish, poultry, legumes, and other healthy food. To make up for the nutrients he may be losing from a food he can't eat, first look to the other foods in the same food group: Are they safe? For instance, the meat and beans food group consists of meat, fish, poultry, eggs, peanuts, tree nuts, seeds, and legumes. If a child is avoiding nuts and eggs, he can still usually meet his nutritional needs by focusing on other foods in the group, like fish and legumes. However, some allergies, like milk, knock out all the foods in the food group. In that case, look for alternatives with the help of a dietician or nutritionist.

IS THERE SOMETHING THAT MAKES SOMEONE MORE PRONE TO FOOD ALLERGIES?

People who develop food allergies tend to have parents or siblings who also have food allergies and/ or allergic conditions such as asthma, hay fever, or eczema. Studies show that 7 percent of fraternal twins and two-thirds of identical twins share peanut allergy, which tells us not only that genes play a big role but also that environment can factor into whether a person develops a food allergy. So, some of the environmental conditions such as indoor air pollution (dust mites, secondhand smoke, mold) and outdoor air pollution (smog, car exhaust) that trigger asthma may also contribute to increased susceptibility to food allergies.

WHY ARE FOOD ALLERGIES INCREASING?

There are many theories. The main one revolves around our ultrahygienic modern world. Our immune systems are designed to fight infections, but there just aren't as many to fight anymore. So, some scientists hypothesize that our immune systems are "looking for a fight" and attacking harmless proteins, like those in food.

Eric Levin, M.D., President/Medical Director of Neponset Valley Pediatrics in Sharon, Massachusetts; Clinical Instructor of Pediatrics, Boston University School of Medicine; Adjunct Staff, Department of Community Medicine, Children's Hospital of Boston.

Marion Groetch, M.S., R.D., C.D.N, Senior Dietitian, Jaffe Food Allergy Institute, Mount Sinai School of Medicine, New York, New York.

Jennifer S. Kim, M.D., Assistant Professor of Pediatrics, Pediatric Allergy and Immunology, Mount Sinai School of Medicine, New York, New York.

Robyn O'Brien, founder of AllergyKids Foundation and author of *The Unhealthy Truth*.

Scott H. Sicherer, M.D., Professor of Pediatrics, Clinician and Clinical Researcher, Jaffe Food Allergy Institute, Mount Sinai School of Medicine, New York, New York, and author of *Understanding and Managing Your Child's Food Allergies* and *The Complete Peanut Allergy Handbook*.

Michael J. Welch, M.D., Codirector, Allergy and Asthma Medical Group and Research Center; Clinical Professor, University of California, San Diego School of Medicine; Editor of *American Academy of Pediatrics Guide to Your Child's Allergies and Asthma: Breathing Easy and Bringing Up Healthy, Active Children*.

breakfast

GOOD MORNING, time for the most important meal of the day! What, everyone's still asleep—or running around looking for the homework that's due today? For families, a healthy, sane, allergy-friendly morning meal can feel as elusive as that math worksheet that's gone missing. But with the right arsenal of ingredients and recipe ideas, you can lose that A.M. stress—or at least decrease it *a lot.*

Experts do insist that breakfast is crucial for kids, whose brains are still developing and who need to have sustained energy for a busy day at school. But when whole-grain cereal or peanut butter on toast aren't an option, what can you put on the plate (or, let's be honest, stick in your child's hand on his way out the door) to make sure your child will get the most out of his morning classes? In this chapter, you'll find tasty, hearty breads and muffins with gluten-free flours, and wholesome, filling quick meals with other allergy-friendly ingredients like flaxseed and rice milk. These will give your kids the protein, fiber, and other nutrients they need to get from your door, through math and reading, and into the cafeteria for a healthy lunch.

When it comes to (slightly) more leisurely weekend mornings, your kids can help you make any of these recipes, which the whole family is sure to enjoy. You won't find better biscuits or French toast at a local diner, and you certainly won't find them minus standard ingredients like all-purpose flour or eggs!

It's time to embrace breakfast again: no guilt, no stress, just a happy, healthy start to the day.

KEY

G=GLUTEN-FREE

D=DAIRY-FREE

N=NUT-FREE

E=EGG-FREE

S=SOY-FREE

Apple Cinnamon Swirl Bread D, N, E, S 3

Banana Bread Waffles G, D, N option, E, S 5

Blueberry Corncakes G, D, N, E, S 6

Breakfast On-the-Go Tacos G option, D, N, E, S 7

Brown Rice Breakfast Pudding G, D, N, E, S 8

Green Eggs and Ham Breakfast Casserole, G, D, N 9

Carrot Cake Breakfast Cookies D, N, E, S 10

Gluten-Free Granola G, D, N option, E, S 12

Individual Egg-Free Frittatas G, D, N, E 13

Quinoa Maple Crunch G, D, N, E, S 14

Autumn Buckwheat and Flax Porridge G, D, E, S 15

Strawberry Rhubarb Muffins G, D, S 16

Tofu Scramble with Spinach G, D, N, E 19

Farmhouse Buttermilk Biscuits and Gravy G, N 20

Super Sweet Potatoes G, D option, N option, E, S 23

Yogurt–Sesame Sweet Potatoes G, D option, N, E, S 24

Oaty Nut Crumble Sweet Potatoes G option, D, N, E, S 25

Frankenstein Sweet Potatoes G, D, N, E, S 26

Sundaes for Breakfast G option, D, N option, E, S 28

Chickpea Soldier Dippers G, D, N, S 30

Fresh Almond or Rice Milk G, D, N option, E, S 31

French Toast Kebabs G option, D, N, E 33

Banana Chocolate Shakeroo G, D, N option, E, S 34

apple cinnamon swirl bread

Apples, cinnamon, and brown sugar—this bread is full of all the stuff warm, cozy break-fasts are made of. And since it's made with fiber-filled whole-wheat flour and flaxseed, it won't cause blood sugar spikes or midmorning hunger pangs. Smear a freshly toasted slice with cream cheese, or nut or seed butter, and head on out the door.

ingredients

- 6 **tablespoons soy-free, nonhydrogenated margarine, at room temperature, plus more for coating the pan**
- 2 **cups whole-wheat pastry flour**
- 2 **teaspoons baking powder**
- 2 **teaspoons ground cinnamon**
- ½ **teaspoon salt**
- ⅔ **cup packed brown sugar**
- 1 **tablespoon ground flaxseed whisked with 2 tablespoons warm water**
- 1 **teaspoon vanilla extract**
- ¾ **cup unsweetened applesauce**
- 1 **Granny Smith apple, peeled and diced**
- 2 **tablespoons dark molasses**
- 1½ **tablespoons unsweetened rice milk, or any other nondairy milk**

PREP TIME: 10 minutes
COOK TIME: 45-50 minutes

1. Preheat the oven to 350°F. Lightly coat a 9 by 5-inch loaf pan with margarine.

2. In a medium bowl, combine the flour, baking powder, cinnamon, and salt. Set aside.

3. In a large bowl, use a mixer to beat the margarine on medium speed for 2 to 3 minutes, until fluffy. Add the brown sugar, and beat 1 minute longer. Add the flaxseed mixture, vanilla, and applesauce and beat again on medium speed until well-combined.

4. Slowly add the dry ingredients to the wet, using a mixer on medium speed to combine. The batter will be a little bit sticky.

5. Scoop out ¼ cup of the batter and place in a small bowl. Fold the diced apple into the remaining batter and spoon into the prepared loaf pan.

6. Add the molasses and milk to the reserved batter and mix well. Pour over the batter in the loaf pan, and use a butter knife, chopstick, or toothpick to form swirls in the batter.

7. Bake for 45 to 50 minutes, until a toothpick inserted into the center comes out clean. Cool completely before turning out of the pan and slicing.

MAKES 10 SLICES
PER SLICE: calories 235, fat 8 g, protein 3 g, carbohydrates 46 g, dietary fiber 4 g

banana bread waffles

Crisp on the outside, chewy on the inside, and filled with banana goodness all throughout, these gluten-free waffles stand up to any wheat variety with gusto. Make fresh to enjoy (with plenty of maple syrup!) on a lazy Saturday morning, or whip up a batch and freeze. Refrigerated in an airtight container, waffles will keep for one day. If you'd like to make more, just double the recipe.

ingredients

- 1 cup brown rice flour
- ¾ cup tapioca flour
- 2 tablespoons raw cane sugar
- 2 teaspoons baking powder
- ½ teaspoon xanthan gum
- 1½ teaspoons ground cinnamon
- ¼ teaspoon ground nutmeg
- ½ teaspoon salt
- 2 very ripe medium bananas, mashed
- ¼ cup canola oil, plus more for brushing the waffle iron
- 1 teaspoon vanilla extract
- 1¼ cups unsweetened almond or rice milk
- ⅓ cup walnuts, chopped (optional)

    Maple syrup

    Extra sliced bananas (optional)

PREP TIME: 5 minutes
COOK TIME: 15 to 20 minutes, depending on your waffle iron

1. Preheat your waffle iron according to the manufacturer's directions. Preheat your oven to 200°F, and set out a rimmed baking sheet.

2. In a large bowl, combine the brown rice flour, tapioca flour, sugar, baking powder, xanthan gum, cinnamon, nutmeg, and salt. Set aside.

3. In a medium bowl, combine the bananas, canola oil, vanilla, and milk. Add to the dry ingredients and mix until just combined. Fold in the walnuts, if using.

4. Use a pastry brush or paper towel to thoroughly oil the top and bottom plates of your waffle iron. Ladle ½ cup of batter onto the iron, and cook according to the manufacturer's directions. Place the waffle on the baking sheet and keep warm in the oven while you make the remaining waffles. Serve warm with maple syrup and extra sliced bananas, if desired.

5. Stack leftover cooled waffles with a sheet of parchment paper in between each one, then place in an airtight container and freeze for up to 1 month.

MAKES 6 WAFFLES
PER WAFFLE: calories 333, fat 15 g, protein 4 g, carbohydrates 48 g, dietary fiber 3 g

blueberry corncakes

These are like your child's favorite pancakes—but heartier. Cornmeal adds welcome texture and crunch to these fruity flapjacks, which taste extra yummy when drizzled with pure maple syrup. Feeding a crowd? The recipe doubles easily.

ingredients

2   **cups finely ground yellow cornmeal**

2   **teaspoons baking powder**

½   **teaspoon salt**

2   **tablespoons ground flaxseed whisked with ¼ cup warm water**

2   **cups unsweetened rice milk**

2   **tablespoons pure maple syrup**

2   **tablespoons canola oil, plus more for coating the pan**

1   **cup blueberries, thawed if frozen**

MAKES 10 CORNCAKES
PER CORNCAKE:
calories 167, fat 5 g,
protein 3 g,
carbohydrates 30 g,
dietary fiber 3 g

PREP TIME: 10 minutes
COOK TIME: 10 to 15 minutes

1. In a large bowl, combine the cornmeal, baking powder, and salt. Set aside.

2. In a medium bowl, combine the flaxseed mixture, rice milk, maple syrup, and canola oil.

3. Add the wet ingredients to the dry and fold together until just combined.

4. Heat the canola oil in a large nonstick skillet over medium heat. Drop the batter in ⅓-cup measures into the skillet, two or three at a time. Sprinkle a few blueberries onto the surface of each corncake.

5. Cook the corncakes for 2 to 3 minutes on the first side, until the bottom seems firm (they won't bubble on the surface as much as traditional pancakes). Flip, then cook for 1 to 2 minutes longer.

6. Serve hot, or cool and freeze (stack cooled corncakes between sheets of parchment paper and store in an airtight container), for up to 1 month. Corncakes can be reheated in the toaster.

breakfast on-the-go tacos

Quick! The bus will be here in no time flat—and everyone's still getting dressed. Your plan of action: Whip up a no-cook filling for portable breakfast tacos that you can hand off to your child while she runs out the door—and rest assured she'll stay energized all morning long, thanks to protein-rich black beans, creamy avocado, and fiber-filled whole-grain tortillas.

ingredients

- 1 **(16-ounce) can black beans, rinsed and drained**
- 1 **ripe avocado, pitted, peeled, and cubed**
- 1 **tablespoon olive oil**
- 1 **teaspoon ground cumin**
- **Juice of ½ lime**
- **Salt**
- 4 **(10-inch) corn or whole-wheat tortillas**

SERVES 4

PER SERVING: calories 355, fat 13 g, protein 13 g, carbohydrates 50 g, dietary fiber 12 g

PREP TIME: 5 minutes

1. Combine the black beans, avocado, olive oil, cumin, and lime juice in a bowl. Season with salt to taste and toss well.

2. Divide the mixture among the tortillas, fold the edges together, and serve. These can be wrapped in foil to eat on the go.

brown rice breakfast pudding

Why serve rice pudding after a meal when you can serve it as a meal instead? Kids and grown-ups will love the balance of sweet maple syrup with tart cranberries in this hearty breakfast porridge. The creamy texture comes courtesy of the starch in the rice.

ingredients

2   **cups uncooked short-grain brown rice**

4   **cups unsweetened rice milk**

3½ **cups water**

2   **tablespoons pure maple syrup**

Pinch of salt

½   **cup dried cranberries**

SERVES 6
PER SERVING: calories 125, fat 1 g, protein 3 g, carbohydrates 31 g, dietary fiber 3 g

PREP + COOK TIME: 1 hour

1. In a medium heavy-bottomed saucepan, combine the rice, rice milk, water, maple syrup, and salt. Bring to a boil, then decrease the heat to low. Simmer, stirring often, for about 50 minutes, until the rice is tender and most of the liquid is absorbed.

2. Add the cranberries and cook for 5 minutes longer. Serve hot, with additional rice milk or maple syrup, if desired. The pudding can be stored in an airtight container for 2 to 3 days, then reheated over low heat, with some rice milk or water added.

green eggs and ham breakfast casserole

This spin on the traditional breakfast casserole uses waffles instead of bread, which adds a hint of sweetness that pairs nicely with the smoked turkey. Best of all, the fun color comes from vitamin-packed spinach, not food coloring. Your kids will like green eggs and ham, they will, they'll like them, Sam I am!

ingredients

Canola oil, for coating the baking dish

2   cups baby spinach (about 3 ounces)

8   large eggs

Pinch of salt

4   gluten-free waffles, toasted and cut into quarters

2   ounces turkey ham or smoked turkey, chopped

SERVES 6
PER SERVING: calories 184, fat 7 g, protein 11 g, carbohydrates 14 g, dietary fiber 1 g

PREP TIME: 20 minutes
COOK TIME: 40 minutes

1.   Preheat the oven to 300°F and coat a 9-inch square baking dish with canola oil.

2.   Steam the spinach until just wilted, then drain well and transfer to a food processor. Pulse until the spinach is roughly chopped. Add 2 of the eggs and the salt and let the processor run until the spinach is completely pureed and the egg mixture looks green, about 30 seconds.

3.   With the processor running, add the remaining 6 eggs through the feed tube, one at a time. After all the eggs are added, continue to run the processor 30 seconds longer.

4.   Spread out the waffles evenly in the baking dish. Sprinkle the turkey over the waffles, then pour the egg mixture over. Bake, uncovered, for 35 to 40 minutes, until set. Let the casserole rest for 5 minutes before serving.

carrot cake breakfast cookies

What kid wouldn't say yes to dessert first thing in the morning? Loaded with fiber, protein, fruit, and veggies, plus low in sugar and fat, you'll feel good about feeding this chewy, cinnamon-spiked cookie to your family for breakfast. For even more staying power, serve alongside a hard-boiled egg or smeared with your favorite nut or seed butter.

DAIRY-FREE

NUT-FREE

EGG-FREE

SOY-FREE

ingredients

- ⅓ cup canola oil, plus more for coating the baking sheets
- 1½ cups whole-wheat pastry flour
- 1½ teaspoons ground cinnamon
- 1 teaspoon ground ginger
- 1 teaspoon baking powder
- ½ teaspoon salt
- ¼ teaspoon ground nutmeg
- ½ cup raw cane sugar
- 1 tablespoon ground flaxseed whisked with 2 tablespoons warm water
- 1 very ripe medium banana, mashed
- 1 cup coarsely grated carrots
- 1 cup old-fashioned rolled oats
- ½ cup pumpkin seeds

PREP TIME: 10 minutes
COOK TIME: 15 to 18 minutes

1. Preheat the oven to 350°F. Lightly coat two baking sheets with canola oil.

2. In a medium bowl, combine the flour, cinnamon, ginger, baking powder, salt, and nutmeg. Set aside.

3. In a large bowl, combine the canola oil and sugar and mix well. Add the flaxseed mixture, banana, and carrots and mix again.

4. Gently fold the dry ingredients into the wet until just combined. Fold in the oats and pumpkin seeds.

5. Use a ⅓-cup measure to scoop five cookies onto each baking sheet, for a total of 10. Bake for 15 to 18 minutes, until golden-brown on the edges.

6. Allow the cookies to sit on the baking sheets for 5 minutes before transferring to a wire rack to cool completely. Serve, or store in an airtight container for 3 to 4 days.

MAKES 10 COOKIES
PER COOKIE: calories 234, protein 4 g, fat 9 g, carbohydrates 40 g, dietary fiber 5 g

GLUTEN-FREE

DAIRY-FREE

NUT-FREE
OPTION

EGG-FREE

SOY-FREE

gluten-free granola

Packed with sugar and fat, most store-bought granolas are desserts masquerading as health foods. This granola cuts way back on both offending ingredients, yielding a mildly sweet mix with a satisfying crunch. If you prefer it a bit sweeter, add a drizzle of honey or maple syrup over individual servings. You might even try this recipe as an ice cream topping. Oats are naturally gluten-free; however, some are processed on equipment that's also used for wheat. When cooking or baking sans gluten, make sure the label specifies that your oats are gluten-free, or processed in a gluten-free facility.

ingredients

- 4 **cups gluten-free rolled oats**
- 1 **cup raw pumpkin seeds**
- ¾ **cup ground flaxseeds**
- 1 **teaspoon ground cinnamon**
- ½ **teaspoon salt**
- ½ **cup pure maple syrup**
- ½ **cup unsweetened applesauce**
- ¼ **cup canola oil**
- 1 **cup dried apricots, chopped**

MAKES ABOUT 6 CUPS
PER ⅓-CUP SERVING:
calories 184, protein 4 g,
fat 7 g, carbohydrates 38 g,
dietary fiber 6 g

PREP TIME: 5 minutes
COOK TIME: 30 minutes

1. Preheat the oven to 325°F.

2. In a large bowl, toss the oats, pumpkin seeds, flaxseeds, cinnamon, and salt to combine.

3. Mix the maple syrup, applesauce, and canola oil in a large mixing cup. Pour over the oat mixture, and stir well, ensuring all of the oats are covered.

4. Divide the granola evenly among two rimmed baking sheets and spread out in a single layer. Bake for 30 minutes, or until crispy and golden-brown, tossing the mixture and rotating the pans halfway through.

5. Once the granola has cooled completely, add the dried apricots. Serve, or transfer to an airtight container. The granola will keep for 1 week.

VARIATIONS

This granola is infinitely adaptable—just keep the fruit and nut/seed proportions the same. Some other delicious combos are:

Cherry and almond

Walnut and fig

Raisin and sunflower seed

individual egg-free frittatas

When baked, firm tofu develops a custardy consistency and texture that's similar to eggs (and hard for kids or grown-ups to resist). Tahini adds richness, while onion, garlic, and lemon provide savory flavor. The turmeric gives a bright yellow color, but is entirely optional if you don't mind a white frittata. Eat alongside toast, or stack in between English muffins with tomato, cheese, or bacon for a quick breakfast sandwich.

ingredients

1	tablespoon olive oil, plus more for coating the muffin cups
1	medium onion, chopped
1	clove garlic, minced
2	cups baby spinach
1	pound firm tofu, drained
¼	cup tahini
1	teaspoon ground turmeric (optional)
1	teaspoon salt
	Juice of 1 small lemon

MAKES 8 FRITTATAS

PER FRITTATA: calories 98, fat 9 g, protein 8 g, carbohydrates 5 g, dietary fiber 2 g

PREP TIME: 15 minutes
COOK TIME: 30 minutes

1. Preheat the oven to 400°F. Lightly coat 8 standard muffin cups with olive oil.

2. Heat the olive oil in a medium sauté pan over medium heat. Add the onion and cook for 5 to 7 minutes, until soft and translucent. Add the garlic and baby spinach and cook for 1 to 2 minutes longer, until the spinach is wilted. Transfer to a medium bowl and set aside.

3. Use your hands to break the tofu into large pieces. Place the tofu in a food processor along with the tahini, turmeric, if using, the salt, and lemon juice. Process until smooth.

4. Add the tofu mixture to the onion mixture and stir to combine. Use a spoon to divide among the 8 prepared muffin cups.

5. Bake for 30 minutes, or until the edges of the frittatas are golden-brown. Allow to sit for 2 to 3 minutes before removing from the muffin tins. Frittatas can be served immediately or at room temperature. Covered in the fridge, they'll last for up to 1 week.

quinoa maple crunch

Boxed cereals tend to be loaded with sugar, and they almost always contain at least one major allergen in the ingredient list (especially gluten, soy, or dairy). Your child will love the crunchy texture and toasty flavor of this homemade version, while you'll love that it's packed with fiber and protein—and is totally allergen-free.

ingredients

- 2   **tablespoons canola oil, plus more for coating the baking sheets**
- 2   **cups quinoa, cooked (makes 4 cups)**
- ⅔   **cup pure maple syrup**
- 2   **teaspoons vanilla extract**
- ¼   **teaspoon salt**
- ½   **teaspoon ground nutmeg**

PREP TIME: 5 minutes
COOK TIME: 50 to 60 minutes

1. Preheat the oven to 325°F. Lightly coat two rimmed baking sheets with canola oil.

2. In a large bowl, combine the quinoa, maple syrup, canola oil, vanilla, salt, and nutmeg.

3. Place half the quinoa on each of the two baking sheets. Use a spatula to spread the mixture evenly across each baking sheet.

4. Bake, stirring frequently with a spatula, for 50 to 60 minutes, until crunchy and golden-brown.

5. Allow the quinoa to cool completely on the baking sheets. Crumble into pieces and serve like cereal, with your child's favorite milk. Store in an airtight container for up to 1 week.

SERVES 8
PER SERVING: calories 272, fat 5 g, protein 6 g, carbohydrates 54 g, dietary fiber 3 g

autumn buckwheat and flax porridge

Earthy buckwheat and flaxseeds ensure this hearty breakfast dish will provide a power-packed start to your child's day, while sweet apricots, peaches, and honey guarantee she'll lick her bowl clean. If you buy your flaxseeds whole, you can grind them down in a clean coffee grinder right before using them.

ingredients

½   **cup raw buckwheat**

1½ **cups unsweetened almond milk**

1½ **cups water**

¼   **teaspoon salt**

3   **tablespoons finely chopped dried apricots**

1   **large peach, or ¾ cup thawed frozen peaches, coarsely chopped**

½   **teaspoon ground cinnamon**

3   **tablespoons honey**

2   **tablespoons ground flaxseeds**

SERVES 4
PER SERVING: calories 206,
fat 5 g, protein 5 g,
carbohydrates 39 g,
dietary fiber 5 g

PREP + COOK TIME: 20 minutes

1. Grind the buckwheat in a food processor until you have a mostly fine powder (it's okay if there are some bigger chunks, as long as all whole kernels are broken down). Fluff with a fork or whisk to break up any lumps.

2. Combine the milk, water, and salt in a small saucepan over medium heat and bring to a simmer. Decrease the heat to medium-low, and add the apricots and peach. Let simmer for 3 minutes while stirring constantly.

3. Slowly add the ground buckwheat to the pan, whisking constantly to break up any lumps as they form. Simmer for 1 minute, whisking constantly.

4. Turn off the heat, cover the pan, and let sit for 10 minutes, whisking every few minutes.

5. Stir in the cinnamon and honey. Fold in the flaxseeds just before eating. Serve immediately, adding more honey or milk to taste.

strawberry rhubarb muffins

These portable, protein-packed muffins will wake up your kids' taste buds first thing in the morning. If organic strawberries and rhubarb are in season, buy them fresh from the farmers' market. Otherwise, frozen will work just as well since you must freeze the fresh produce to create a more baking-friendly texture.

ingredients

- ¾ **cup fresh or frozen strawberries, chopped fine**
- ¼ **cup fresh or frozen rhubarb, chopped fine**
- 2 **cups almond flour**
- ½ **teaspoon salt**
- ½ **teaspoon baking soda**
- 2 **large eggs, beaten**
- ¼ **cup honey, plus extra for drizzling**

PREP TIME: 10 minutes
COOK TIME: 30 minutes

1. If using frozen strawberries and rhubarb, defrost, drain, chop, and mix together. If using fresh strawberries and rhubarb, mix chopped produce, spread on a parchment-lined rimmed baking sheet, and freeze for 6 hours, then defrost and drain.

2. Preheat the oven to 325°F. Line 8 standard muffin cups with paper liners.

3. Combine the almond flour, salt, and baking soda in a medium bowl. Set aside.

4. Add the eggs to a large bowl and slowly drizzle in the honey, whisking as you go to combine evenly.

5. Slowly pour the dry ingredients into the eggs and honey, mixing well. Add the fruit and stir to combine.

6. Using a small ladle, fill the muffin cups about three-quarters full. Stir the batter in the bowl after filling each cup so the fruit does not settle to the bottom.

7. Bake for 30 minutes, or until the tops become lightly golden-brown. Allow the muffins to rest in the pan for 3 minutes, then transfer to a cooling rack.

8. Serve warm with additional honey for drizzling.

VARIATIONS

For strawberry-peach muffins, use ½ cup strawberries and replace the rhubarb with ½ cup coarsely chopped fresh or frozen peaches.

For blueberry muffins, replace the strawberries and rhubarb with 1 cup whole fresh or frozen blueberries.

For chocolate chip muffins, replace the fruit with ¾ cup chocolate chips. Use a sharp knife to chop up your chips to a finer texture before mixing into the batter.

MAKES 8 MUFFINS
PER MUFFIN: calories 287, fat 20 g, protein 14 g, carbohydrates 17 g, dietary fiber 4 g

tofu scramble
with spinach

Can't eat eggs or just tired of them? Scrambled tofu is another savory breakfast option with a similar, custardlike consistency and satisfying protein punch. Perhaps even better, it cooks up super quick, and tastes great alongside toast and potatoes, or scooped into tortillas. If you don't have turmeric on hand, don't worry—the spice is mostly used to give the tofu a yellow color.

ingredients

PREP TIME: 5 minutes
COOK TIME: 12 to 15 minutes

2	**tablespoons olive oil**
1	**small yellow onion, diced**
2	**cloves garlic, minced**
1	**pound firm tofu, drained**
2	**tablespoons wheat-free tamari**
1	**teaspoon ground turmeric (optional)**
	Juice of ½ lemon
2	**large handfuls baby spinach (about 4 cups)**

1. In a large skillet, heat the olive oil over medium heat. Add the onion and garlic and sauté for 5 to 7 minutes, until soft and translucent.

2. While the onion cooks, prep the tofu. With your fingers, crumble the tofu into a large bowl. Add the tamari, turmeric, if using, and lemon juice and toss, mashing lightly with a fork.

3. Add the tofu mixture to the pan and cook, stirring frequently, for 5 minutes, until the pieces of the tofu have browned slightly and most of the moisture has cooked out. Add the spinach and stir until wilted, then remove from the heat and serve.

SERVES 6

PER SERVING: calories 95, fat 9 g, protein 10 g, carbohydrates 4 g, dietary fiber 2 g

farmhouse buttermilk biscuits and gravy

A standard gluten-free flour blend of brown rice flour, potato starch, and tapioca gets a little help from the fluffy textures of sorghum flour and sweet rice flour for this recipe. Served with a creamy gravy of mushrooms and savory spices, these biscuits are a hearty weekend breakfast dish that's a welcome change from the usual pancakes or waffles. Please note that this recipe calls for potato starch, not potato flour.

ingredients

GLUTEN-FREE FLOUR MIX

½ **cup brown rice flour**

⅓ **cup potato starch**

5 **tablespoons tapioca starch**

BISCUITS

¾ **cup gluten-free flour mix, plus more for rolling out dough**

3 **tablespoons sweet rice flour**

3 **tablespoons sorghum flour**

1 **tablespoon raw cane sugar**

2 **teaspoons baking powder**

½ **teaspoon baking soda**

¼ **teaspoon xanthan gum**

3 **tablespoons cold butter, cut into 12 small chunks**

3 **tablespoons cultured buttermilk**

3 **tablespoons cold water**

1 **large egg white**

PREP TIME: 15 minutes
COOK TIME: 40 minutes

1. To make the gluten-free flour mix, sift together the brown rice flour, potato starch, and tapioca starch in a medium bowl. Set aside.

2. Preheat the oven to 400°F. Line a medium rimmed baking sheet with parchment paper.

3. To make the biscuits, sift together ¾ cup of the gluten-free flour mix, sweet rice flour, sorghum flour, sugar, baking powder, baking soda, and xanthan gum in a medium bowl. Cut in the cold butter with a pastry blender or two forks until it resembles a coarse meal. Place the bowl in the refrigerator while you complete the next two steps.

4. Mix together the buttermilk and water in a cup and set aside.

5. In a large bowl, beat the egg white with a mixer on medium speed for about 1 minute, until foamy enough to barely form soft peaks.

6. Pour the buttermilk mixture and the refrigerated butter mixture into the egg white all at once, mixing with a fork until well-combined.

MUSHROOM GRAVY

2	tablespoons olive oil
1	medium yellow onion, chopped
2	cups trimmed and quartered crimini mushrooms
3	cloves garlic, diced
4½	cups low-sodium vegetable broth
2	tablespoons fresh lemon juice
4	tablespoons wheat-free tamari
	Salt and freshly ground black pepper
5	fresh sage leaves, chopped
2	teaspoons fresh thyme leaves
¼	cup cold water
3	tablespoons cornstarch
4	tablespoons butter

7. Lay down a piece of parchment on the counter and spread out a handful of gluten-free flour mix. Pat the biscuit dough into a thick, flat layer and divide it into 8 equal parts. Using your hands, form round biscuits that are about 2½ inches in diameter and about 1 inch thick.

8. Place the biscuits on the prepared baking sheet, about 1 inch apart. Bake for 23 to 26 minutes, until the tops are just beginning to turn golden-brown.

9. To make the mushroom gravy, heat the olive oil in a large sauté pan over medium-low heat until it shimmers. Add the onion and cook, stirring occasionally to prevent burning, for about 10 minutes, until sweet-smelling and just beginning to turn brown.

10. Add the mushrooms to the onion and cook, stirring occasionally, for about 12 minutes, until the mushrooms are soft. Add the garlic and continue cooking for 2 minutes longer. Remove the onion, mushrooms, and garlic to a bowl and set aside.

continued on page 22

11. Turn the heat to medium under the same pan you used for the onion and mushrooms. Add the vegetable broth, lemon juice, and tamari. Using a spatula, deglaze the pan while bringing the liquid to a simmer. Add ½ teaspoon pepper, the sage, and thyme. Lower the heat to medium-low, and cook, stirring occasionally, for about 20 minutes, until the sauce has thickened somewhat.

12. In a cup, mix the water and cornstarch with a fork until all the lumps are broken up. Slowly pour the cornstarch slurry into the simmering gravy, whisking quickly the whole time to distribute the cornstarch. Continue to simmer, stirring constantly, for 3 to 5 minutes, until the gravy thickens. Add the butter and stir until melted and completely mixed in. Remove from the heat and season with salt and pepper to taste. Pour over the warm biscuits and serve.

VARIATIONS

For more savory biscuits, mix ¾ teaspoon dried sage into the dry ingredients before cutting in the butter.

For sweeter biscuits, increase the sugar by 2 teaspoons and add 1 extra teaspoon of buttermilk.

For fruity-flavored biscuits, replace the water with an equal amount of filtered apple juice or other filtered, nonacidic fruit juice.

MAKES 8 SERVINGS
PER SERVING: calories 319, fat 14 g, protein 5 g, carbohydrates 43 g, dietary fiber 1 g

super sweet potatoes

Sweet potatoes just might be the perfect breakfast food. They're loaded

with energy-sustaining complex carbohydrates and are a good source of

fiber plus vitamins A and C. When topped with protein-rich yogurt, beans,

or chopped nuts, they're bound to keep you going all morning. Bake your

sweet potatoes in the oven the night before at 400°F for 45 minutes to

1 hour, and reheat the next morning in the microwave for 2 to 3 minutes.

Alternatively, microwave them in the morning for 6 to 10 minutes until

fork-tender. Load up with toppings, wrap the whole thing in foil to stay

warm, and head out the door for a healthy meal on the run.

yogurt-sesame sweet potatoes

The Middle Eastern–inspired topping is chock-full of calcium and protein, thanks to the yogurt and sesame seeds. The tangy yogurt balances out the rich sweetness of the potatoes, while the sesame seeds add crunch.

ingredients

2 **cups plain, low-fat yogurt or coconut milk yogurt**

¼ **cup sesame seeds**

1 to 2 tablespoons honey

4 **medium sweet potatoes, baked and reheated, if necessary**

PREP TIME: 5 minutes

In a medium bowl, add the yogurt, sesame seeds, and honey to taste. Stir to combine, and divide the topping among the four sweet potatoes.

SERVES 4

PER SERVING: calories 263, fat 7 g, protein 10 g, carbohydrates 43 g, dietary fiber 5 g

oaty nut crumble sweet potatoes

If your family has ever craved sweet potato pie for breakfast, topping baked potatoes with this nutty, buttery crumble just might satisfy them. For an extra-special treat, slide the topped potatoes in the toaster oven for a few minutes to make the crumble warm and crispy.

ingredients

- ⅓   **cup whole-wheat pastry flour or brown rice flour**
- ¼   **cup gluten-free rolled oats**
- 3   **tablespoons brown sugar**
- 2   **tablespoons canola oil**
- ¼   **teaspoon salt**
- ¼   **teaspoon ground cinnamon**
- ⅛   **teaspoon ground ginger**
- 4   **medium sweet potatoes, baked and reheated, if necessary**

SERVES 4

PER SERVING: calories 245, fat 8 g, protein 4 g, carbohydrates 47 g, dietary fiber 6 g

PREP TIME: 5 minutes

In a medium bowl, add the flour, oats, brown sugar, canola oil, salt, cinnamon, and ginger. Mix with a fork, and divide the topping among the four sweet potatoes.

frankenstein sweet potatoes

The orange, black, and green colors make this breakfast perfect for serving around Halloween—but the tasty combo of creamy black beans and avocado will make you want to serve these up year-round.

ingredients

1   **(16-ounce) can black beans, rinsed and drained**

1   **avocado, pitted, peeled, and cubed**

   Juice of ½ lime

   Salt

4   **medium sweet potatoes, baked and reheated, if necessary**

PER SERVING: calories 324, fat 7 g, protein 13 g, carbohydrates 54 g, dietary fiber 17 g

PREP TIME: 5 minutes

In a medium bowl, add the black beans, avocado, lime juice, and salt to taste. Toss gently, and divide the topping among the four sweet potatoes.

teach your child
how to bake a sweet potato

Sweet potatoes are easy to bake, if your child knows the secret trick: Piercing the potatoes with a fork before baking releases excess steam, making for a perfectly soft, moist spud.

STEP 1 Fruits and veggies should always be washed before eating, especially sweet potatoes, which grow underground. Have your child run each potato under warm water, and use his hands or a clean scrub brush to wipe away any visible dirt. Then, he can wipe them dry with a kitchen towel.

STEP 2 Help your child use a fork to carefully poke a couple of holes in each sweet potato. Sweet potatoes contain a lot of water, and it's important to let some of the steam escape when they cook.

STEP 3 Wrap each sweet potato individually in foil. That way, all the steam that escapes from the holes will stay close by, keeping the skin from drying out while it cooks.

STEP 4 Help your child place the foil-wrapped potatoes on a baking sheet and into the oven. Bake for 45 minutes to 1 hour, then remove. When the foil is cool enough to touch, test for doneness by inserting a toothpick or butter knife into each sweet potato. If it goes in smoothly, the potatoes are ready! If not, wrap them up again and stick them back in the oven.

sundaes for breakfast

What better way to get kids to eat good-for-them yogurt and fruit than dressed up as a fun-to-eat parfait of creamy yogurt, crunchy granola, and juicy fruit? Serve them in sundae glasses on special mornings, or layer in mason jars and top with a lid for a portable breakfast.

ingredients

- ½ **cup plain, low-fat yogurt, or coconut milk yogurt**
- ¼ **cup Gluten-Free Granola (page 12) or your favorite allergy-free, store-bought granola**
- ½ **medium banana, sliced**
- ¼ **cup fresh or frozen raspberries, plus 1 raspberry, reserved**
- 2 **teaspoons honey**
- 1 **teaspoon unsweetened coconut flakes**

MAKES 1 SUNDAE

PER SUNDAE: calories 351, fat 11 g, protein 12 g, carbohydrates 54 g, dietary fiber 6 g

PREP TIME: 10 minutes

In a sundae glass or pint-size mason jar, add one-third of the yogurt, then one-third of the granola, and top with one-third of the bananas and raspberries. Drizzle with some of the honey. Repeat twice more, creating three layers total. Add the coconut flakes, and top with the reserved raspberry. Serve.

chickpea soldier dippers

Usually, sliced rectangles of toast are dunked into soft-boiled eggs. This updated, gluten-free version uses chickpea flour to make rich, chewy dippers that kids will love just as much. Plus, they're packed with plenty of fiber, protein, and complex carbs to keep kids full all morning long. If you have any left over, these also are delicious dipped into Mighty Marinara Sauce (page 56).

ingredients

2½ **cups water**

2 **tablespoons olive oil, plus more for coating the pan**

2 **cups chickpea flour, sifted**

½ **teaspoon salt**

Soft-boiled eggs, for serving

SERVES 8

PER SERVING: calories 119, fat 5 g, protein 5 g, carbohydrates 13 g, dietary fiber 3 g

PREP TIME: 1 to 2 hours
COOK TIME: 25 minutes

1. In a medium saucepan, bring the water to a boil. Lightly coat an 8-inch square baking dish with olive oil.

2. In a medium bowl, mix the chickpea flour and salt to combine. Slowly add the chickpea flour mixture to the boiling water, whisking as you go. Add the olive oil. Lower the heat to low and cook for 1 to 2 minutes longer, until the mixture has thickened.

3. Pour the chickpea mixture into the prepared pan, using a spatula to smooth the top. Refrigerate for 1 to 2 hours, or until the mixture is firm.

4. Preheat the oven to 400°F. Lightly coat a rimmed baking sheet with olive oil.

5. Turn the cooled batter out onto a clean surface. Slice the toast into 4 strips one way and 8 strips the other way, making 32 rectangles.

6. Place the rectangles on the prepared baking sheet. Bake for 25 minutes, or until golden-brown. Cool for 2 to 3 minutes. Serve with the soft-boiled eggs.

fresh almond or rice milk

Admittedly, both almond and rice milk are easy enough to find at most grocery stores—but the homemade stuff is infinitely fresher, creamier, and all-around tastier than any boxed variety. Plus, you can avoid the unnecessary added sugar found in many store-bought, nondairy milks.

ingredients

1   cup whole raw almonds or long-grain brown rice, or a combination of both

½   teaspoon vanilla extract

½   teaspoon ground cinnamon (optional)

    Pinch of salt

4   cups water, divided

MAKES 4 CUPS

PER CUP OF ALMOND MILK:
calories 103, fat 9 g,
protein 4 g,
carbohydrates 4 g,
dietary fiber 2 g

PER CUP OF RICE MILK:
calories 40, fat 0 g,
protein 1 g,
carbohydrates 8 g,
dietary fiber 1 g

PREP TIME: 5 minutes, plus 8 hours unattended

1. Place the almonds or rice in a medium bowl with enough water to cover. Cover, and let sit for 8 hours or overnight.

2. Drain the almonds or rice and rinse thoroughly.

3. In a blender, add the almonds or rice, vanilla, cinnamon, if using, and salt. Add 1 cup of the water and blend on high for about 1 minute, until the mixture is somewhat smooth.

4. Add the remaining 3 cups of water and blend again until thoroughly combined and as smooth as possible.

5. Pour through a fine-mesh strainer or cheesecloth to remove any large pieces of almond or rice. Serve, or refrigerate covered for up to 2 days.

french toast kebabs

You'd be hard-pressed to find a kid (or grown-up) who doesn't love French toast. Our version of the spiced breakfast favorite is made even more fun served on skewers with sliced fruit, and it's made with silken tofu to get that egg-y custard coating everyone loves.

ingredients

- 12 **ounces soft silken tofu, drained**
- 2 **tablespoons raw cane sugar**
- 1 **teaspoon ground ginger**
- 1 **teaspoon vanilla extract**
- ½ **teaspoon salt**
- ¼ **teaspoon ground nutmeg**
- 3 **tablespoons canola oil**
- 8 **slices whole-wheat bread or gluten-free bread, crusts removed**
- 2 **cups assorted sliced fruit, such as bananas, grapes, strawberries, and pineapple**
- 8 **bamboo skewers**

MAKES 8 KEBABS

PER KEBAB: calories 166, fat 8 g, protein 5 g, carbohydrates 21 g, dietary fiber 2 g

PREP + COOK TIME: 30 minutes

1. Place the tofu, sugar, ginger, vanilla, salt, and nutmeg in a food processor, and puree until completely smooth. Pour the mixture into a wide, shallow bowl.

2. Heat 1½ tablespoons of the canola oil in a large nonstick skillet over medium heat.

3. Dip each slice of bread into the tofu mixture, coating the top and bottom. Place half of the coated slices in the pan. Cook for 3 to 4 minutes, until lightly browned on one side, flip, and cook for 2 to 3 minutes longer on the other side. Keep the cooked slices warm in a 200°F oven.

4. Add the remaining 1½ tablespoons of canola oil to the pan and cook the remaining bread slices.

5. When cool enough to touch, slice each piece of French toast into 6 squares. Place 6 squares on each skewer, alternating with pieces of fruit.

GLUTEN-FREE

DAIRY-FREE

NUT-FREE
OPTION

EGG-FREE

SOY-FREE

banana chocolate shakeroo

Meet the fastest breakfast around. In about the time it'll take your child to brush her teeth, you can whip up this rich, chocolaty meal-in-a-glass (or reusable bottle) to give her as she heads out the door. For multiple smoothies, just double or triple the ingredients.

ingredients

PREP TIME: 2 minutes

1   **large frozen banana, cut into chunks**

¾   **cup unsweetened almond or rice milk**

1   **tablespoon tahini**

1   **tablespoon cocoa powder**

1   **teaspoon honey**

⅛   **teaspoon ground cinnamon**

Place the banana, milk, tahini, cocoa powder, honey, and cinnamon in a blender. Blend on high until smooth. Serve.

SERVES 1

PER SERVING: calories 278, fat 12 g, protein 6 g, carbohydrates 45 g, dietary fiber 7 g

five fun ways to serve fruit

If your child tends to pass over the berries and orange wedges that are so healthy at breakfast (or anytime), worry no more. These super-easy techniques will turn plain old fruit into an exciting way to start the day.

FRUITY POTATO HEAD Don't worry—there are no actual potatoes involved! On a plate, arrange fruit pieces to form a face à la the famous spud. Try sliced kiwifruit for eyes, grapes or cherries for the nose, and peach slices for a mouth. Then get creative with the details: What can your child use to make a mustache? Ears and earrings? Eyebrows or hair? For a more substantial snack or meal, put the fruit on a slice of whole-wheat bread or bagel that's been spread with nut or seed butter or cream cheese.

SWEET BREAKFAST SANDWICH Tucked in between whole-wheat pancakes, waffles, or French toast, plain sliced fruit becomes extra appealing.

DRINK FLOATIES Drop berries, sliced grapes, chopped apples, or orange wedges into water or club soda to add flavor (plus tons of vitamins, antioxidants, and fiber).

MINI KEBABS Toothpicks make the perfect snack-size skewers for little hands—and are a surprise at breakfast. Use a combination of whatever seasonal fruit is available, such as apples and pears or strawberries and blueberries. This option is best for kids 3 years old and up.

FRUIT CUPPERS Make an ordinary Wednesday a celebration by filling a cupcake wrapper with fruits that aren't too wet, like blueberries, cherries, or raspberries. Increase the treat factor with a dusting of powdered sugar or a sprinkle of mini chocolate chips.

lunch

NOTHING KEEPS the afternoon cranky kid monster away better than a healthy lunch. And nothing keeps the all-day cranky *mom* monster away better than easy, yummy ideas for what to make.

We've given some old favorites an allergy-friendly twist: Who needs PB&J when you can have Almond Butter-n-Apple 'Wiches? You'll forget all about frozen pizza pockets when you've tried our gluten-free version. We've also gathered together some fresh flavors that'll keep lunchtime fun. Did you know you could make falafel with edamame and "sushi" with cauliflower? Beyond the cool factor is this: They taste delicious.

And since packing lunch is one of the biggest pains in any parent's life—not to mention the parent of a child who can't even go near the school lunch line—many of these recipes can be packed up and sent in your child's lunch box. He won't even *want* to trade them away for stuff he can't eat.

When you're shopping for lunchtime staples and making a plan for the week (or for today; we're not *all* that organized), keep in mind that the key to a balanced lunch is pulling from three categories: protein, carbohydrate, and fruits and vegetables. And the key to a happy lunch is not stressing if you miss one of those categories some days. You'll make it up tomorrow!

KEY

G=GLUTEN-FREE

D=DAIRY-FREE

N=NUT-FREE

E=EGG-FREE

S=SOY-FREE

Almond Butter-n-Apple 'Wiches G option, D, E, S 39

No-Cream of Broccoli Soup G, D, N, E, S 40

Cheddar Avocado Quesadilla G option, N, E, S 41

Edamame Carrot Falafel Pitas G option D, E 43

Eggplant, Tomato, and Mozzarella Circles G, N, E, S 44

Corn Chowder with Red Pepper Confetti G, N, E, S 45

World's Best Kale Salad G, D, N, E 46

Pizza Pockets G, N, E, S 47

Gluten-Free Pizza Dough G, D, N, E, S 48

Sweet Summer Corn Salad G, D, N, E, S 50

Veggie Bite Soup G, D, N, E, S 53

Tomato and Grilled Cheese Soup G option, N, E, S 55

Mighty Marinara Sauce G, D, N, E, S 56

Edamame, Carrots, and Shells G option D, N, E 57

Garden Wrap-n-Rolls G, D option, N, E, S 58

Glazed Mini Meat Loaf Muffins G, D, N, S 60

Egg Salad and Ham Sandwich Sticks G option, N, S 63

Butternut Squash and Zucchini Pancakes G, D option, N, S 64

Barbecue Chicken Salad G, D, N, E 66

Veggie Sushi Bites G, D, N, E option 68

Lemony Tuna Salad on Cucumber Slices G, N, E option, S 70

almond butter-n-apple 'wiches

Need lunch fast? This speedy sandwich is a yummier spin on your kid's favorite PB&J, and it's healthier, to boot. Almond butter is higher in protein than traditional peanut butter, and slices of whole apples are higher in fiber and antioxidants—plus lower in sugar—than the standard grape jelly.

ingredients

- 1 **apple, peeled and thinly sliced**
- 1 **teaspoon fresh lemon juice**
- ¼ **teaspoon ground cinnamon**
- 4 **tablespoons almond butter**
- 4 **slices whole-wheat or gluten-free bread**

MAKES 2 SANDWICHES

PER SANDWICH: calories 494, fat 23 g, protein 13 g, carbohydrates 65 g, dietary fiber 9 g

PREP TIME: 5 minutes

1. In a small bowl, add the apple slices, lemon juice, and cinnamon. Toss to combine, and set aside.

2. Spread 2 tablespoons of the almond butter on 2 of the bread slices. Top each of the slices with half of the apple slices, and cover with the remaining 2 bread slices.

3. Slice each sandwich in half. Serve, or pack one in a reusable food container or food wrapper and stick inside your child's lunch box.

no-cream
of broccoli soup

Broccoli's strong flavor can be a tough sell to most kids—but this pale green soup's sure to please eaters of all ages. Sweet Yukon gold potatoes add creaminess and substance, nixing the need for dairy. Serve alongside your favorite whole-grain bread (wheat or gluten-free) for dunking.

ingredients

PREP TIME: 10 minutes
COOK TIME: 30 minutes

2	**tablespoons olive oil**
1	**large yellow onion, diced**
2	**cloves garlic, minced**
1	**pound Yukon gold potatoes, diced**
1	**pound broccoli crowns (tough ends removed), chopped**
4	**cups vegetable broth**
	Salt and freshly ground black pepper

1. In a large pot, heat the olive oil over medium-high heat. Add the onion and sauté for 5 to 7 minutes, until soft and translucent. Add the garlic and cook 1 minute longer.

2. Add the potatoes, and sauté, stirring frequently, for about 3 minutes, until they just begin to brown. Add the broccoli and sauté for 1 to 2 minutes longer.

3. Add the vegetable broth. Cover, bring to a boil, then simmer for 15 to 20 minutes, until the broccoli and potatoes have softened completely.

4. Working in batches, carefully add the soup to a blender and puree until smooth. If you have an immersion blender, now's a great time to use it, as you can blend the soup right in the pot. If needed, return the soup to the pot and simmer for 5 minutes longer, until hot. Season to taste with salt and pepper and serve.

SERVES 4

PER SERVING: calories 200, fat 7 g, protein 7 g, carbohydrates 33 g, dietary fiber 7 g

cheddar avocado quesadilla

You might not think to put high-protein cheese and *creamy avocado into a quesadilla, since both ingredients are on the rich side, but the combination is a must-try. The monounsaturated fat from the avocado supports heart health, and when eaten with the cheddar, will guarantee your child is satisfied all the way until dinner. Pair these flattened sandwiches alongside some baby carrots or celery sticks for a quick lunch.*

ingredients

- 1 **teaspoon canola oil**
- 1 **(10-inch) whole-wheat or brown rice flour tortilla**
- ¼ **cup shredded cheddar cheese**
- ¼ **avocado, sliced**
- 1 **tablespoon of your favorite salsa**

SERVES 1

PER SERVING: calories 360, fat 23 g, protein 12 g, carbohydrates 30 g, dietary fiber 7 g

PREP + COOK TIME: 5 to 7 minutes

1. Heat ½ teaspoon of the canola oil in a skillet over medium-high heat. Lay the tortilla on a flat surface. Spread the cheddar cheese over half the tortilla, add the avocado slices, and top with the salsa. Fold in half.

2. Use a pastry brush to brush the top half of the quesadilla with the remaining ½ teaspoon of canola oil.

3. Use a spatula to transfer the quesadilla to the pan, oiled side up. Place a second, clean skillet on top of the quesadilla and cook for 1 to 2 minutes, until golden-brown and crispy.

4. Remove the top skillet, flip the quesadilla, and cook for 1 to 2 minutes longer. Serve hot.

edamame carrot falafel pitas

Traditional chickpea falafel requires a deep-fryer, plus soaking the chickpeas for 24 hours before you even start cooking. This edamame version comes together in under an hour, and it's just as tasty in pita pockets as in salads, or even subbed for meatballs over your favorite pasta. When packing these pockets for lunch, store the Tahini-Lime Sauce in a separate container for your child to add right before she eats. That way, the pita won't get soggy.

ingredients

Canola oil, for coating the baking sheet

1   cup shelled edamame, thawed if frozen

½   cup chopped carrots

½   small onion, quartered

½   cup walnuts

2   tablespoons tahini

1   clove garlic

    Juice of ½ lime

½   teaspoon ground cumin

¾   teaspoon salt

4   whole-wheat or gluten-free pita pockets

1   red bell pepper, chopped

1   cucumber, peeled and chopped

½   medium head red cabbage, thinly sliced

Tahini-Lime Sauce

PREP TIME: 20 minutes
COOK TIME: 25 minutes

1. Preheat the oven to 425°F. Lightly coat a rimmed baking sheet with canola oil.

2. In a food processor, combine the edamame, carrots, onion, and walnuts until finely chopped. Add the tahini, garlic, lime juice, cumin, and salt and process until well-mixed.

3. Form the mixture into 12 golf ball–size balls. Place on the prepared baking sheet, and bake for 15 minutes, until lightly browned. Flip, bake for 10 minutes longer, then remove from the oven and let cool.

4. Assemble the pita pockets. Place 3 falafel balls in each pita, then top with the bell pepper, cucumber, and cabbage. Drizzle with 1 to 2 tablespoons of the sauce and serve.

MAKES 4 SANDWICHES
PER SANDWICH: calories 320, fat 15 g, protein 14 g, carbohydrates 39 g, dietary fiber 8 g

TO MAKE THE TAHINI-LIME SAUCE, combine ¼ cup tahini, the juice of ½ lime, plus salt to taste in a small bowl. Stir, adding enough water (2 to 4 tablespoons) to make a thin sauce. Refrigerated in an airtight container, the sauce will keep for up to 1 week.

MAKES 4 SERVINGS
PER SERVING: calories 91, fat 8 g, protein 3 g, carbohydrates 4 g, dietary fiber 1 g

eggplant, tomato, and mozzarella circles

These gooey, veggie-rich rounds prove you don't need bread to make a delicious sandwich. The recipe calls for a large, conventional eggplant, but you could also use a thinner, Japanese-style eggplant to make mini sandwiches for a kid-friendly snack.

ingredients

1 **large eggplant, sliced into 12 (½-inch-thick) rounds**

¼ **cup olive oil**

Salt

⅓ to ½ **cup Mighty Marinara Sauce (page 56), or your favorite jarred sauce**

⅔ **cup shredded mozzarella cheese**

6 **basil leaves, sliced into ribbons**

SERVES 6

PER SERVING: calories 152, fat 12 g, protein 4 g, carbohydrates 7 g, dietary fiber 3 g

PREP TIME: 20 minutes
COOK TIME: 12 minutes

1. Preheat the oven to 425°F. Set out a rimmed baking sheet.

2. Place the eggplant slices on the baking sheet. Use a pastry brush to brush each slice with olive oil. Flip, and brush the other sides and sprinkle with salt.

3. Bake the eggplant slices for 7 to 9 minutes, or until they are beginning to brown and soften. Allow to cool for 5 minutes, or until cool enough to touch.

4. Spread 1 to 2 tablespoons of the marinara sauce on 6 eggplant slices, then top each of the slices with 2 tablespoons of mozzarella cheese. Add the basil, then top with the other 6 eggplant slices.

5. Bake for 3 to 4 minutes longer, until the cheese has melted. Serve warm.

corn chowder
with red pepper confetti

Cutting the red peppers into tiny squares gives this rich chowder a festive appearance that kids will love. For extra fun, put your child in charge of garnishing her own bowl—she can toss the red pepper squares and basil strips into her soup like party confetti.

ingredients

PREP TIME: 10 minutes
COOK TIME: 20 minutes

1	tablespoon olive oil
1	medium sweet onion, diced
1½	pounds Red Bliss potatoes, unpeeled, diced (about 4 cups)
6	cups vegetable broth
4	cups fresh or frozen corn
3½	cups whole milk, divided
3	tablespoons cornstarch
1	medium red bell pepper, finely diced (about 1 cup)
¼	cup finely chopped basil
	Salt and freshly ground black pepper

1. Heat the oil in a large heavy-bottomed stockpot over high heat. Add the onion and cook for about 5 minutes, until browned at the edges and beginning to soften. Add the potatoes and stir to combine. Add the broth and bring to a boil. Decrease the heat to medium-low, and simmer for about 10 minutes, until the potatoes are tender.

2. Add the corn and 3 cups of the milk and bring to a boil. In another small bowl, whisk together the cornstarch and the remaining ½ cup of milk. Add this slurry to the soup and return to a boil, stirring often. Add the bell pepper and basil, and season to taste with salt and pepper. Serve immediately.

SERVES 6
PER SERVING: calories 300, fat 8 g, protein 10 g, carbohydrates 50 g, dietary fiber 6 g

world's best kale salad

Okay, we know what you're thinking: My kid, eat KALE? *It's true, the nutrient-packed green's bitterness is unappealing to most children (and plenty of adults, too). But this salad just might change everyone's mind. Use your hands to rub the kale leaves with the rich, creamy, and slightly sweet dressing to soften them and massage the bitterness into submission. It's a bit of a messy job—in other words, one kids will probably love. Hearty kale leaves store well, even after they've been dressed, making this an easy-to-pack lunch.*

ingredients

1 **bunch curly kale, stems and ribs removed, leaves sliced into ribbons**

2 **medium carrots, peeled and chopped**

¼ **cup tahini**

2 **tablespoons yellow miso**

1 **tablespoon fresh lemon juice**

1 **teaspoon pure maple syrup**

¼ **cup warm water**

SERVES 6

PER SERVING: calories 129, fat 6 g, protein 5 g, carbohydrates 17 g, dietary fiber 5 g

PREP TIME: 15 minutes

1. Place the kale and carrots in a large bowl, and toss to combine. Set aside.

2. In a small bowl, add the tahini, miso, lemon juice, and maple syrup. Slowly whisk in the water until the mixture is completely smooth.

3. Pour the dressing over the salad. Use your hands to toss, coating the salad completely and massaging the dressing into the leaves.

4. Let sit for 5 to 10 minutes to allow the dressing to wilt the kale slightly. Serve.

pizza pockets

Now, gluten-free eaters can have the same frozen sandwich pockets that all their friends eat. The perfectly crispy crust makes for a satisfying contrast against the gooey, melty cheese, guaranteeing a thumbs-up review from your kid. Make a double batch, if you'd like, to store a bunch in the freezer for quick meals. To freeze, wrap cooled pizza pockets individually in foil, then store in a zip-top bag for up to 1 month.

ingredients

Olive oil, for coating the baking sheet

1 batch Gluten-Free Pizza Dough (page 48), or your favorite gluten-free pizza dough

Rice flour, for dusting

¾ cup Mighty Marinara Sauce (page 56), or your favorite jarred sauce

¾ cup shredded mozzarella cheese

½ cup grated Pecorino Romano or Parmesan cheese

¼ cup unsweetened rice milk

MAKES 4 PIZZA POCKETS
PER PIZZA POCKET:
calories 473, fat 15 g,
protein 16 g,
carbohydrates 55 g,
dietary fiber 4 g

PREP TIME: 10 minutes
COOK TIME: 10 minutes

1. Preheat the oven to 500°F. Lightly coat a rimmed baking sheet with olive oil.

2. Divide the pizza dough into 4 equal pieces. On a surface dusted with rice flour, roll each of the 4 dough pieces into a circle, about 8 inches. The dough should be ⅛ to ¼ inch thick.

3. Spread 3 tablespoons of the marinara sauce on half of each dough circle. Top each with 3 table-spoons of mozzarella cheese and 2 tablespoons of the Pecorino Romano or Parmesan cheese, then fold over and crimp shut the edges with fingers or a fork.

4. Use a pastry brush to lightly brush each pizza pocket with rice milk (you may have some left over). Use a paring knife to score three small slits on the top of each pizza pocket.

5. Use a spatula to transfer the pizza pockets to the baking sheet. Bake for 10 minutes, or until the crust begins to brown. Serve hot. Pizza pockets also can be frozen and reheated to enjoy later. To reheat, thaw, then bake in a 350°F oven for 15 to 20 minutes, until heated through on the inside and crisp on the outside.

gluten-free
pizza dough

Please note that this recipe calls for potato starch, not potato flour.

ingredients

- 1¼ teaspoons active dry yeast
- ¾ cup warm water
- 1 tablespoon plus pinch of raw cane sugar
- ¾ cup chickpea flour, sifted
- ½ cup brown rice flour
- ½ cup potato starch
- ½ cup tapioca flour
- 2¼ teaspoons xanthan gum
- 1 teaspoon salt
- 1 tablespoon olive oil, plus more for coating a large bowl

**MAKES ENOUGH DOUGH FOR
4 PIZZA POCKETS, OR 1 PIZZA**
PER ¼ RECIPE: calories 318,
fat 5 g, protein 5 g,
carbohydrates 61 g,
dietary fiber 3 g

PREP TIME: 10 minutes
RISING TIME: 1 hour

1. In a small bowl, combine the yeast with ¼ cup of the water and a pinch of sugar. Set aside for 5 to 10 minutes, until the yeast begins to froth.

2. In a large bowl, add the chickpea flour, brown rice flour, potato starch, tapioca flour, xanthan gum, salt, and the remaining 1 tablespoon of sugar. Mix well to combine.

3. Add the yeast mixture to the flour mixture, then add the remaining ½ cup of water and the olive oil. Stir or mix with your hands to form a sticky ball. Place the dough in a large bowl that's been lightly coated with olive oil, cover the dough with a kitchen towel, and leave in a warm place to rise for 1 hour, or until doubled in size.

COOKING WITH KIDS

teach your child
to roll out pizza dough

(Successfully) handling pizza dough might seem intimidating—but it's actually so easy, a kid can do it! With these simple steps, your kid will be rolling like a pro in no time flat.

STEP 1   After your dough has risen to double its original size, have your child punch it down into the bowl. Explain that pizza dough expands because of the yeast: The yeast "burps" after eating the sugar, creating extra air that causes the dough to get bigger.

STEP 2   With your child, get ready to roll the dough by dusting a rolling pin and a clean countertop with flour. Point out that the extra flour will keep the dough from getting stuck on any surfaces.

STEP 3   Together, flatten the dough into a disk. Demonstrate the rolling technique by pushing the rolling pin down into the dough, then away from you. Repeat, occasionally rotating the dough to roll out a circle. Hold onto the rolling pin with your child and try rolling together a few times, then let him try on his own. Continue until you've created a circle that's the size you want.

STEP 4   Carefully lift the pizza dough onto your prepared baking sheet. If it tears, don't worry: Show your kid how to fix the rip by grabbing a small piece of dough from the edge of the circle and patching the hole.

sweet summer corn salad

The tastiest version of this picnic-perfect meal-in-a-bowl is made with peak-season corn and tomatoes. Visit a local farm stand with your child to pick up the vegetables, and prepare for the taste of summer: sweet veggies, creamy avocado, and tangy lime. Pack with an ice pack in your child's lunch box for a cool, refreshing lunch.

ingredients

- 3 **tablespoons olive oil**
- 2 **cups yellow or white corn (from about 4 ears)**
- 1 **clove garlic, minced**
- 1 **(16-ounce) can black beans, rinsed and drained**
- 1 **large tomato, seeded and chopped**
- ½ **small red onion, diced**
- 2 **tablespoons chopped cilantro**
- ½ **teaspoon ground cumin**
- ½ **teaspoon chili powder**
  Juice of 1 lime
  Salt and freshly ground black pepper
- 1 **large avocado, pitted, peeled, and cubed**

PREP TIME: 20 minutes

1. Heat 1 tablespoon of the olive oil in a large skillet over high heat. When the oil is shiny, add the corn in an even layer and let sit untouched for 2 to 3 minutes, until browned on one side. Stir to combine, add the garlic, and sauté for 2 minutes longer. Remove from the heat and set aside.

2. In a large bowl, add the black beans, tomato, red onion, cilantro, cumin, chili powder, lime juice, and the remaining 2 tablespoons olive oil. Add the corn and salt and pepper to taste, and toss until well-mixed. Add the avocado and toss gently, taking care not to mush the avocado.

3. Serve warm or at room temperature, alone or with your favorite tortilla chips.

SERVES 6
PER SERVING: calories 225, fat 12 g, protein 7 g, carbohydrates 26 g, dietary fiber 8 g

COOKING WITH KIDS

teach your child
how to juice and zest a lime

STEP 1 Have your child wash a lime and dry it thoroughly with a clean cloth.

STEP 2 Let your child roll the lime on the counter while pressing firmly with his palm. Explain to your child that this is to get the lime juicier for when he squeezes it later.

STEP 3 With a citrus zester, show your child how to scrape some of the zest off of the lime's rind by gliding the zester in one direction over the green part of the lime. Tell your child that he wants to scrape off just the green part, not the bitter white part that's underneath it. Although you'll need only a little of the zest, encourage your child to practice by zesting as much as he likes. Let your child rub the zest between his fingers and smell the citrusy scent. Explain that the zest gives food even more delicious lime flavor.

STEP 4 After you slice the lime in half with a sharp serrated knife, let your child squeeze the juice out of the lime and into a small bowl or measuring cup. You can use a manual citrus squeezer, citrus press, wooden reamer, or an electric juicer.

STEP 5 Let your child taste the lime juice by dipping a spoon in it. Explain that sour is one of the four main taste senses along with sweet, salty, and bitter. He has thousands of tiny taste buds on his tongue to react to the flavors of food. (Your child may want to take a peek at his tongue in a mirror.) Let your child measure the juice with a measuring spoon to see how juicy the lime is.

veggie bite soup

Carrots, peas, parsnips, and tomato sauce come together to make a mild, sweet soup that big or little eaters will love. If your quinoa doesn't specify that it's already been rinsed, be sure to run the seeds under cold water in a fine-mesh strainer. It'll remove the naturally occurring soapy-tasting coating (called saponins) that deters animals from eating quinoa in the wild.

ingredients

2	**tablespoons olive oil**
1	**large yellow onion, diced**
1	**large carrot, peeled and diced**
1	**celery stalk, diced**
2	**parsnips, peeled and diced**
2	**cloves garlic, minced**
1	**cup frozen green peas**
½	**cup quinoa**
6	**cups vegetable broth**
¾	**cup tomato sauce**
	Salt and freshly ground black pepper

SERVES 6

PER SERVING: calories 120, fat 5 g, protein 2 g, carbohydrates 18 g, dietary fiber 3 g

PREP TIME: 15 minutes
COOK TIME: 35 minutes

1. In a large stockpot, heat the olive oil over medium heat. Add the onion and sauté for 5 to 7 minutes, until soft and translucent. Add the carrot, celery, parsnips, and garlic, and sauté for 5 to 7 minutes longer.

2. Add the peas, quinoa, vegetable broth, and tomato sauce and stir well to combine. Cover and bring to a boil, then reduce the heat.

3. Simmer the soup for about 20 minutes, until the quinoa is fully cooked. Season to taste with salt and pepper and serve.

tomato and grilled cheese soup

Soup and a sandwich? This classic combo gets an update with cheesy crouton bites dropped right into a bowl of steamy, creamy tomato soup. It's especially comforting on cold days— like after your kids come in from playing in the snow.

ingredients

4	tablespoons olive oil
1	medium yellow onion, diced
2	cloves garlic, minced
1	carrot, peeled and diced
1	teaspoon dried thyme
1	bay leaf
1	tablespoon tomato paste
1	(28-ounce) can crushed tomatoes, with juice
2	cups vegetable broth
8	slices whole-wheat or gluten-free bread, crusts removed
2	cups (16 ounces) shredded cheddar cheese
1½	cups unsweetened rice milk
	Salt and freshly ground black pepper

PREP TIME: 10 minutes
COOK TIME: 30 minutes

1. Preheat your broiler. Set out a rimmed baking sheet.

2. In a large stockpot, heat 1 tablespoon of the olive oil over medium heat. Add the onion and sauté for 5 to 7 minutes, or until soft and translucent. Add the garlic, carrot, thyme, and bay leaf and sauté for 5 to 7 minutes longer, until the vegetables have softened.

3. Add the tomato paste, tomatoes, and vegetable broth. Bring the mixture to a boil, then reduce the heat and simmer for 20 minutes, or until the soup has thickened slightly.

4. Place the bread slices on the baking sheet and brush with the remaining 3 tablespoons of olive oil. Turn the slices over and top each with ¼ cup cheddar cheese. Broil for 3 to 5 minutes, until the cheese is bubbly and the bread is lightly toasted.

5. While the bread toasts, add the rice milk to the soup and stir well. Remove the bay leaf and season to taste with salt and pepper.

6. Make four sandwiches with the bread slices, and slice each sandwich into 8 cubes.

7. Ladle the soup into bowls, topping each with 4 grilled cheese cubes. Serve.

SERVES 8
PER SERVING: calories 326, fat 19 g, protein 14 g, carbohydrates 28 g, dietary fiber 6 g

mighty marinara sauce

This punched-up tomato sauce is brimming with fresh, flavorful veggies—but since they're chopped so finely, picky eaters won't even notice them. Enjoy it in many of our recipes such as Pizza Pockets, or use for pasta, lasagne, or even as a dipping sauce.

ingredients

1   **tablespoon olive oil**

1   **large onion, quartered**

1   **clove garlic**

1   **large carrot, peeled and quartered**

1   **stalk celery, quartered**

1   **(28-ounce) can crushed tomatoes**

   Salt

1   **bay leaf**

PREP TIME: 10 minutes
COOK TIME: 30 minutes

1. In a large stockpot, heat the olive oil over medium heat.

2. In a food processor, combine the onion, garlic, carrot, and celery. Process until very finely chopped.

3. Add the vegetables to the stockpot and sauté for 5 to 7 minutes, until soft and translucent.

4. Add the tomatoes and season with salt to taste. Bring to a boil, then lower the heat to a simmer and add the bay leaf. Simmer, partially covered, for about 30 minutes, until the flavors are well-blended. Remove the bay leaf and serve.

SERVES 6
PER SERVING: calories 83, fat 3 g, protein 3 g, carbohydrates 15 g, dietary fiber 4 g

edamame, carrots, and shells

The best part about this tangy Asian-inspired pasta salad? The surprise bites that come from the tiny carrot pieces and edamame that get cocooned inside some of the pasta shells—which kids always seem to get excited about. Plus, it's super fast to make and can be eaten hot or cold.

ingredients

12 **ounces whole-wheat or gluten-free medium pasta shells**

¼ **cup wheat-free tamari**

2 **tablespoons toasted sesame oil**

2 **tablespoons rice wine vinegar**

2 **tablespoons honey**

2 **medium carrots, peeled and diced**

2 **cups shelled edamame, thawed if frozen**

3 **tablespoons sesame seeds**

PREP TIME: 10 minutes
COOK TIME: 7 to 10 minutes

1. Bring a large pot of water to a boil and cook the shells according to the package directions.

2. While the shells cook, combine the tamari, sesame oil, rice wine vinegar, and honey in a large serving bowl. Whisk to combine.

3. About 1 minute before the shells are ready, add the diced carrots and edamame to the boiling water. Cook 1 minute longer, then drain.

4. Add the shells, carrots, and edamame to the serving bowl and toss with the tamari mixture to coat. Garnish with the sesame seeds. Serve hot, cold, or at room temperature.

SERVES 6

PER SERVING: calories 360, fat 9 g, protein 15 g, carbohydrates 57 g, dietary fiber 7 g

garden
wrap-n-rolls

Your kid will jump at the chance for an interactive meal, where he fills cool, crunchy lettuce leaves with this summer-inspired fare. Pack the salad and lettuce leaves separately for a school lunch. For a dairy-free version, chopped olives give the same salty bite as feta cheese.

ingredients

PREP + COOK TIME: 50 minutes

1   **cup French lentils, picked over and rinsed**

1   **large carrot, peeled and grated**

1   **red bell pepper, diced**

1   **yellow bell pepper, diced**

½   **cup finely chopped fresh parsley**

3   **tablespoons olive oil**

2   **cloves garlic, minced**

¼   **cup crumbled feta cheese or chopped black olives**

    Salt and freshly ground black pepper

8 to 10 **butterhead or romaine lettuce leaves**

SERVES 4

PER SERVING: calories 210, fat 13 g, protein 8 g, carbohydrates 19 g, dietary fiber 6 g

1. Place the lentils in a medium saucepan with enough water to cover by 1 to 2 inches. Cover and bring to a boil, then simmer, half-covered, for 40 minutes, or until the lentils are cooked through.

2. While the lentils cook, add the carrot, bell peppers, and parsley to a large bowl, and toss to combine.

3. Drain the cooked lentils and rinse under cold water until cool enough to touch. Add to the vegetables and toss to combine.

4. In a small skillet, heat the olive oil over medium-high heat. Add the garlic and sauté, stirring frequently, for about 30 seconds, or until fragrant and just beginning to brown.

5. Pour the garlic and olive oil over the lentils and vegetables. Add the feta cheese or olives and salt and pepper to taste. Toss until well-combined.

6. To serve, scoop the lentil mixture into the lettuce leaves. Fold in half and serve.

CORN CHOWDER WITH
RED PEPPER CONFETTI, PAGE 45

glazed mini meat loaf muffins

Instead of bread crumbs, these meat loaf muffins use heart-healthy oats and feature a sweet, kid-pleasing glaze on top. And while the petite size is easier to bake, it's also extra appealing to little eaters, who can munch on the muffins directly out of hand. They're good cold, too, so you can pack them in a lunch box.

ingredients

MEAT LOAF

2   tablespoons canola oil, plus more for coating the muffin cups

2   large yellow squash, grated on a box grater (about 4 cups)

1   large clove garlic, minced

¾   pound 90 percent lean ground beef sirloin

¾   pound 80 percent lean ground pork

1   teaspoon kosher salt

½   teaspoon freshly ground black pepper

1   large egg

2   tablespoons ketchup

½   cup quick-cooking gluten-free oats

PREP TIME: 20 minutes
BAKE TIME: 30 minutes

1.   For the meat loaf, preheat the oven to 350°F.

2.   In a medium nonstick pan, heat the oil over medium-high heat. Add the squash to the pan, and cook, stirring every 2 minutes, for 8 to 10 minutes, until the squash has softened and reduced by half. Stir in the garlic and cook for 1 minute longer, before removing from the heat. Let cool.

3.   Meanwhile, in a large bowl, add the ground sirloin, ground pork, salt, pepper, egg, ketchup, and oats. Add the squash. Using a spoon or your hands, combine the ingredients well.

4.   Coat 12 muffin cups with canola oil, and pack the meat mixture into 12 cups. Bake for 15 minutes.

GLAZE

⅓ **cup ketchup**

2 **tablespoons yellow mustard**

2 **tablespoons honey**

5. For the glaze, combine the ketchup, mustard, and honey in a small bowl. Remove the meat loaves from the oven, and glaze the top of each with about 1 tablespoon of the glaze. Save the remaining glaze for meat loaf sandwiches.

6. Return the meat loaves to the oven, and cook for 15 minutes longer. Remove from the oven, and cut through one meat loaf to make sure it is cooked through. Cool for a few minutes and serve. Leftover muffins will keep in an airtight container for up to 5 days; the glaze will keep for up to 1 week.

MAKES 12 MEAT LOAF MUFFINS
PER SERVING: calories 175, fat 7 g, protein 20 g, carbohydrates 10 g, dietary fiber 1 g

egg salad and ham sandwich sticks

The secret to the silkiness of this egg salad comes from the cream cheese. Celery adds a crunch—and salty ham makes this sandwich sing. If your kid's not a mayonnaise fan, replace the tablespoon of mayo with sour cream. Worried about packing this one for lunch? Adding an ice pack will keep the sticks chilled and fresh.

GLUTEN-FREE OPTION

NUT-FREE

SOY-FREE

ingredients

- 6 **large eggs**
- 1 **tablespoon mayonnaise, plus extra for sandwiches**
- 2 **ounces cream cheese, at room temperature**
- ¼ **teaspoon salt**
- ¼ **teaspoon freshly ground black pepper**
- 1 **celery stalk, chopped (about ¼ cup)**
- 8 **slices whole-grain or gluten-free bread**
- ⅓ **pound thinly sliced gluten-free honey-glazed ham**

MAKES 6 SERVINGS
(16 TO 20 SANDWICH STICKS)
PER SERVING: calories 224, fat 10 g, protein 15 g, carbohydrates 20 g, dietary fiber 3 g

PREP TIME: 15 minutes
COOK TIME: 10 minutes

1. In a medium pot, add the eggs and fill with enough water to cover the eggs by 1 inch. Bring the water to a boil over high heat.

2. As soon as the water begins to boil, cover the pot with a lid and remove from the heat. Let the eggs sit covered in the hot water for 10 minutes.

3. Carefully drain the hot water, and peel the shells from the eggs.

4. In a small bowl, add the eggs and mash with a fork, or shred the eggs on a box grater. Add the mayonnaise, cream cheese, salt, pepper, and celery; use a spoon to combine. Taste and adjust the seasonings, if needed.

5. Place the bread pieces on a cutting board, and spread the bread with mayonnaise, if desired. Mound the egg salad onto 4 pieces of bread, add 2 to 3 slices of ham onto each, and top with the remaining 4 bread slices. Using a serrated knife, carefully cut into 1-inch sticks, removing the crusts, if desired. Depending on the size of the bread, you should have 4 to 5 sticks per sandwich.

butternut squash and zucchini pancakes

Made with shredded butternut squash and zucchini, these little pancakes are a colorful, portable lunch option. A touch of Indian spices lends a zip to the sweet squash, making for a savory meal that kids can eat with their hands. Keep the pancakes in a warm oven until they are all cooked, then serve with a dollop of plain yogurt and a sprinkling of chopped parsley, if you like. Or, stick them in a reusable container or your child's lunch box for later—they're just as good cold.

ingredients

2   **cups grated zucchini**

2   **cups grated butternut squash**

½   **cup chickpea and fava bean flour (garfava flour)**

¼   **cup finely ground cornmeal**

3   **shallots, minced**

2   **large eggs, beaten**

1   **teaspoon sea salt**

1   **teaspoon freshly ground black pepper**

1   **teaspoon ground cumin**

1   **teaspoon ground turmeric**

¼   **teaspoon ground cinnamon**

3   **tablespoons olive oil**

Chopped fresh parsley, for garnish

Plain or coconut yogurt, for garnish

PREP TIME: 20 minutes
COOK TIME: 30 minutes

1. Dry the grated zucchini by lining the bottom of a rimmed baking sheet with kitchen towels and spreading the zucchini out in a thin layer. Layer another towel on top and gently press down, removing any excess water.

2. In a large bowl, combine the zucchini, squash, garfava flour, cornmeal, and shallots. Mix well and set aside.

3. Beat together the eggs, salt, pepper, cumin, turmeric, and cinnamon in a medium bowl. Using your hands, mix the eggs into the squash mixture until well-combined.

4. Heat 1 teaspoon of the olive oil in a large nonstick skillet over medium heat. Use a large spoon to drop ½ cup of squash batter into the pan and spread it around so that it's about ½ inch thick. Let the pancake cook for 3 minutes, then flip with a spatula and cook the other side for 3 minutes longer. The pancake should be cooked through and both sides should be golden-brown. Keep the pancakes warm in a 200°F oven until all are cooked. Garnish with parsley and yogurt, if desired, and serve.

5. These pancakes can be kept in the refrigerator for 4 days, or in the freezer for up to 1 month. Allow them to cool completely before refrigerating to prevent them from getting soggy.

NOTE: For a sweeter dessert or breakfast pancake, omit the shallots, turmeric, cumin, and pepper, and substitute 3 tablespoons of maple syrup and 2 teaspoons of pumpkin pie spice.

MAKES 5 (6-INCH) PANCAKES
PER PANCAKE: calories 218, fat 11 g, protein 8 g, carbohydrates 23 g, dietary fiber 4 g

barbecue chicken salad

Making your own barbecue sauce is easy, and lets you enjoy it as spicy or sweet as your family likes. We like to think of it as a vehicle to get your child to eat more protein-packed chicken and vitamin-rich greens—but they'll probably find plenty of other things to slather it on, too!

ingredients

PREP TIME: 15 minutes
COOK TIME: 15 minutes

BARBECUE SAUCE

3	tablespoons extra-virgin olive oil
4	shallots, diced
4	teaspoons water
2	cloves garlic, diced
1	(15-ounce) can peaches, drained
1	(8-ounce) can pineapple chunks, drained
1	cup diced tomatoes
¼	cup apple cider vinegar
1	teaspoon freshly ground black pepper
1	teaspoon red pepper flakes
¼	cup wheat-free tamari
¼	teaspoon cayenne pepper
5	tablespoons molasses

1. For the barbecue sauce, add the olive oil and shallots to a small saucepan while it is still cold. Heat the pan over a low flame and cook the shallots, stirring occasionally to keep them from burning, for about 2 minutes, until they begin to caramelize and smell sweet. Add 1 tablespoon of the water and continue to cook, stirring occasionally, for 7 minutes longer, until the shallots are soft. Add the garlic and the remaining 1 teaspoon of water, and cook, stirring constantly, for 3 minutes longer. Remove from the heat.

2. Place the peaches, pineapple, tomatoes, vinegar, pepper, red pepper flakes, tamari, cayenne, molasses, and the shallots and garlic in a blender jar. Pulse until completely smooth. Store in an airtight container for up to 1 week in the refrigerator.

3. For the chicken, season the chicken breasts on both sides with salt and pepper.

4. Heat the olive oil in a large pan over medium heat. Sauté the chicken breasts for about 5 minutes on each side. The chicken is done when the juices run clear and the thickest part of the breast is no longer pink when pierced with a knife.

CHICKEN

2 large boneless, skinless chicken breasts, at room temperature

1 teaspoon salt

½ teaspoon freshly ground black pepper

3 tablespoons extra-virgin olive oil

SALAD

½ head romaine lettuce, trimmed and cut into 1-inch strips

1 large handful baby spinach leaves

1 small handful baby Swiss chard leaves

1 small handful fresh basil leaves, chopped

½ cup whole corn kernels, cooked

1 (15-ounce) can garbanzo beans, rinsed and drained

2 large, ripe heirloom tomatoes, seeded and chopped

½ cup chopped fresh parsley, for garnish

5. Remove the chicken breasts from the heat, and set to cool on a plate. Once cool, slice thinly and set aside.

6. For the salad, toss the greens, corn, garbanzo beans, and tomatoes together in a large bowl. Transfer to individual salad bowls.

7. Top each salad with a few slices of chicken, and drizzle with a generous amount of barbecue sauce. Sprinkle with the chopped parsley and serve.

SERVES 4
PER SERVING: calories 350, fat 20 g, protein 4 g, carbohydrates 41 g, dietary fiber 4 g

veggie sushi bites

Not even kids can resist their veggies when wrapped up in these cute little rolls. The chopped cauliflower makes a neat stand-in for rice—making this dish not only vegetarian-friendly but raw food–friendly, too. And since these bites are fish-free, they pack well for a super-healthy lunch.

ingredients

¼ **large head cauliflower, chopped into florets**

4 **sheets toasted nori (sushi wrappers)**

1 **avocado, pitted, peeled, and cut into narrow strips**

½ **cucumber, peeled and cut into narrow strips about 2 inches long**

1 **small carrot, peeled and finely shredded**

Wheat-free tamari, for dipping

SERVES 4

PER SERVING: calories 119, fat 7 g, protein 4 g, carbohydrates 9 g, dietary fiber 5 g

PREP TIME: 15 minutes
MAKE TIME: 10 minutes

1. Place the cauliflower in a food processor. Process until the cauliflower is chopped fine and resembles rice.

2. Place one sheet of nori on a cutting board. Spread approximately 2 tablespoons of the chopped cauliflower along the bottom third (closest to you) of the nori. Place one-quarter of the avocado and cucumber strips on top of the cauliflower, then sprinkle with one-quarter of the carrot.

3. Dip your fingers in the water and run them across the top ½ inch of the nori to dampen. Start rolling the nori from the bottom so the vegetables are wrapped up inside; wrap as tightly as you can without breaking the nori, then seal along the damp edge with water as needed. Set aside and repeat with the remaining nori sheets and fillings.

4. When all the sheets are rolled, take a sharp knife and cut each roll in half crosswise, then cut each half into three bite-size pieces. Serve with small bowls of tamari for dipping.

lemony tuna salad on cucumber slices

English cucumbers are ideal for these bright-tasting, bread-free sandwiches because they have fewer seeds than other varieties. To send this in a school lunch, pack the tuna and cucumber slices separately and let the kids assemble the sandwiches themselves.

ingredients

3 tablespoons mayonnaise or vegan mayonnaise

Grated zest of 2 lemons

1½ teaspoons fresh lemon juice

½ teaspoon salt

¼ teaspoon freshly ground black pepper

2 tablespoons chopped bread-and-butter pickles

2 (5-ounce) cans tuna in water, drained

1 to 2 English cucumbers, peeled and sliced ¼ inch thick

PREP TIME: 15 minutes
COOK TIME: 10 minutes

1. In a small bowl, add the mayonnaise, lemon zest, lemon juice, salt, pepper, and pickles. Stir to combine.

2. Add the tuna, and combine with the lemon dressing. Taste, and adjust the seasonings, if needed.

3. Assemble the cucumber sandwiches: Spread 1 tablespoon of tuna salad in the middle of 1 cucumber slice and top with a second slice. Repeat with the remaining cucumber slices until all of the tuna has been used. Serve.

MAKES 4 SERVINGS
PER SERVING: calories 130, fat 5 g, protein 17 g, carbohydrates 4 g, dietary fiber 0 g

tips for packing a greener lunch

When it comes to packing lunch, you've got the *healthy* part down pat (whole grains, fruits and veggies, lean proteins, and healthy fats). But what about the green? Here are some easy ideas that'll make your child's lunch more Earth-friendly, and likely save you money, too.

GREEN BAG IT A child who brings lunch in a 6-ounce paper bag every day generates 67 pounds of waste by the end of the school year, according to the EPA. Go from brown to green with a reusable pack.

SAVE THE WRAPPER Fabric sandwich and snack bags are easy to wash and reuse, making them a green alternative to landfill-bound plastic wrap and foil.

WIPE MESSES CLEAN Cloth napkins might not have the ability to turn a kid's cafeteria meal into a civilized affair, but they will slash paper waste.

DRINK GREEN Those stainless-steel bottles are good for more than just water. Purchase juice or iced tea in full-size—rather than single-serve—containers, and portion out a serving for your child's lunch canteen.

FORK OVER THE PLASTIC Afraid your good utensils will end up in the lost-and-found if you pack 'em in your kid's lunch box? Pick up a cheap set of spoons, forks, and knives at your local thrift shop, and say good-bye to disposables forever.

GO WITH NATURE Snacks like apples, oranges, bananas, peaches, and pears come with their own natural wrappers, making them an ideal choice for waste-free lunches. Plus, they're healthier than packaged foods anyway!

PACK THE RIGHT STUFF Make your own cookies, granola bars, and hummus to cut down on packaging from the grocery store (it'll taste fresher and save money, too). When you do buy premade, cut trash by opting for full-size bags or boxes rather than single-serve.

dinner

ALMOST EVERY parent has to grapple with kids who "won't" eat certain foods—and that's a pain. But when you've got a child who actually *can't* eat certain foods, the pressure is really on. Wouldn't it be great to have a stable of recipes that everyone in the family will want to eat—not just the one with an allergy who *has* to eat it? Now you do. These recipes are nutritious, delicious, and safe. No one will feel left out, no one will go searching for something else after dinner's over—and no one will feel like a short-order cook.

Here's the other problem with dinner: Pretty much as soon as you've conquered it and gotten it on the table, you have to start thinking about tomorrow. It's so easy to fall into a rut with the same recipes, especially when you're limited on ingredients—you have a kid who can't eat pasta, or you're a family that has cut out dairy. That's why we've given you a variety of types of dinners here, from franks and beans to sweet potato gnocchi. Many of these recipes also double easily, which means you can freeze the leftovers to save your sanity next week.

One last word about dinner: We hear all the time about how important it is for families to eat together. Kids eat healthier, they get better grades, and they are less likely to smoke or drink. These things are true, and it *is* worth the effort, even if you're able to schedule everyone to be around the table together only two nights each week. But remember: Getting dinner on the table every night is an accomplishment that too often goes unnoticed with the stress that can surround mealtime. So, we'll say it, "Well done, Mom and Dad!"

G=GLUTEN-FREE

D=DAIRY-FREE

N=NUT-FREE

E=EGG-FREE

S=SOY-FREE

KEY

Tofu-Stuffed Shells G option, D, N, E 75

Super Green Pesto Rice Bowl G, D, E, S 76

Southwest Beans and Corn Bread Bake D, N, E, S 78

Buddha Bowls G, D, N, E 80

Franks-n-Beans G, D, N, E 81

Corn Chip–Crusted Tofu Fingers G, N 82

Cool Zucchini Noodles G, D, N, E, S 84

Sweet Potato Gnocchi with Lentils D, N option, E, S 86

Mac-n-Cheeze D, N, E, S 89

Greener Sloppy Joes G option, D, N, E, S 91

Lentil Burgers G option, D, N, E, S 92

Olive Oil Twice-Baked Potatoes G, D, N, E, S 93

Chicken Potpie with Sweet Potato Topping G, D option, N, S 94

Tuna–Brown Rice Bake G, N, E, S option 97

Beef Satay with Peanut Noodles and Snow Peas G, D, E, S 98

Spicy Mexican Shrimp Skewers G, D, N, E, S 101

Cheesy Stuffed Pizza Burgers G option, D option, N, E, S 102

Easy Lemon Chicken G, D, N, E, S 103

All-Day Roast Pork Shoulder G, D, N, E 104

Healthy Turkey Stir-Fry with Broccoli and Cashews G, D, E . . . 106

tofu-stuffed shells

Traditional stuffed shells are filled with a mixture of ricotta cheese, Parmesan, and eggs. Not only does this soy-based version taste just as good, it's also lower in fat and calories.

ingredients

¼   cup olive oil, plus more for coating the baking dish

2   pounds firm tofu, drained

1   teaspoon salt

2   cloves garlic

Juice of 1 lemon

12   basil leaves

12   ounces jumbo pasta shells or gluten-free jumbo pasta shells

2½   cups Mighty Marinara Sauce (page 56), or your favorite marinara sauce

SERVES 4 TO 6

PER SERVING: calories 358, fat 14 g, protein 28 g, carbohydrates 56 g, dietary fiber 7 g

PREP TIME: 20 minutes
BAKE TIME: 30 minutes

1. Preheat the oven to 375°F. Lightly coat a 9 by 13-inch baking dish with olive oil. Bring a large pot of salted water to a boil.

2. In a food processor, add the tofu, oil, salt, garlic, lemon, and basil and process until completely smooth. Transfer to a medium bowl.

3. Cook the shells according to the package directions. Drain and rinse under cold water, then transfer to a rimmed baking sheet or other surface so the cooked shells aren't touching each other. This will prevent them from sticking together.

4. Spread ¼ to ⅓ cup of the sauce evenly across the bottom of the baking dish. Fill each shell with a heaping spoonful of the tofu mixture, then place in the baking dish (you may have some of the tofu mixture leftover at the end).

5. Top the shells with the remaining sauce. Cover with foil and bake for 30 minutes, or until heated through completely. Serve with a green salad or steamed vegetables.

super green pesto rice bowl

Swiss chard and plum vinegar might sound like grown-up ingredients, but combining them with garlic, almonds, and olive oil makes for a cheesy-tasting pesto that'll win over eaters of all ages. Find plum vinegar at natural-food stores or Asian markets.

ingredients

1	**bunch Swiss chard,** stems removed, leaves roughly chopped
½	**cup almonds, toasted**
1	**clove garlic**
1	**tablespoon umeboshi plum vinegar**
¼	**cup plus 1 tablespoon olive oil**
	Salt and freshly ground black pepper
1¼	**cups brown rice**
¾	**pound green beans, trimmed and chopped into 1-inch pieces**
1	**small butternut squash, chopped into ½-inch pieces**

SERVES 6

PER SERVING: calories 320, fat 18 g, protein 9 g, carbohydrates 38 g, dietary fiber 12 g

PREP + COOK TIME: 1 hour

1. Cook the brown rice according to the package directions.

2. While the rice is cooking, preheat the oven to 425°F. Set out a rimmed baking sheet, and bring a large saucepan filled with salted water to a boil. To make the pesto, add the Swiss chard to the boiling water and cook for 1 minute, until tender and bright green. Use tongs to remove the chard from the water, saving the water in the pot, and place the chard in a food processor. Add the almonds, garlic, and plum vinegar. Process until well-combined, then add ¼ cup of the olive oil and process again, until thoroughly mixed. Season to taste with salt and pepper. Set aside.

3. Add the green beans to the boiling water and cook for 3 to 4 minutes, until bright green and just tender. Drain and run under cold water. Add to the bowl of rice.

4. Meanwhile, place the butternut squash pieces on the baking sheet and drizzle with the remaining 1 tablespoon of olive oil. Season with salt. Toss to coat and bake for 15 to 20 minutes, until the squash has softened and the edges are lightly browned.

5. Add the rice, green beans, and squash to a large bowl. Toss with the pesto and serve hot or at room temperature.

southwest beans and corn bread bake

Beans and corn bread usually end up on the table together anyway, so why not combine the two into one clever casserole? Serve it hot from the oven, or make ahead of time and reheat for a busy school night.

ingredients

BEANS

1	tablespoon olive oil
1	medium yellow onion, diced
1	medium red bell pepper, diced
1	large zucchini, diced
½	cup corn (from 1 large ear, or frozen and thawed)
2	cloves garlic, minced
2	teaspoons chili powder
1	teaspoon ground cumin
½	teaspoon smoked paprika
1	(15-ounce) can black beans, rinsed and drained
¾	cup tomato sauce
	Salt and freshly ground black pepper

PREP TIME: 30 minutes
COOK TIME: 20 minutes

1. Preheat the oven to 350°F. Lightly oil a 9-inch round pan.

2. To make the beans, heat the olive oil in a large skillet over medium-high heat. Add the onion and sauté for 5 to 7 minutes, until soft and translucent. Add the bell pepper, zucchini, corn, and garlic and sauté for 5 minutes, until softened. Add the chili powder, cumin, and paprika and sauté for 30 seconds.

3. Add the black beans, tomato sauce, and salt and pepper to taste. Stir to combine and simmer for 5 minutes. Remove from the heat and set aside.

4. To make the corn bread, combine the rice milk and vinegar in a small bowl. Set aside.

5. In a large bowl, add the flour, cornmeal, sugar, baking powder, and salt and mix to combine. Pour the rice milk mixture into the flour mixture, then add the canola oil and fold gently to combine.

CORN BREAD

¾ **cup plus 2 tablespoons unsweetened rice milk**

1 **teaspoon apple cider vinegar**

1 **cup whole-wheat pastry flour**

½ **cup finely ground yellow cornmeal**

1 **tablespoon raw cane sugar**

1 **teaspoon baking powder**

½ **teaspoon salt**

2 **tablespoons canola oil**

SERVES 6

PER SERVING: calories 287, fat 8 g, protein 8 g, carbohydrates 47 g, dietary fiber 9 g

6. Pour the bean mixture into the prepared pan, and use a spatula to smooth out the top. Pour the corn bread batter over the beans, and gently smooth with a spatula.

7. Bake for 17 to 20 minutes, until the corn bread is beginning to turn golden-brown and a toothpick inserted into the center comes out clean. Cool for 5 minutes and serve.

buddha bowls

A sweet, tamari-based sauce makes the veggies in this dish appealing to little eaters. Not a fan of tofu? Substitute an equal amount of organic chicken or beef.

ingredients

1	tablespoon plus 1 teaspoon canola oil, plus more for coating the baking sheet
¼	cup plus 1 tablespoon wheat-free tamari
1	tablespoon rice wine vinegar
1	tablespoon honey
1	teaspoon toasted sesame oil
1	clove garlic, minced, or 1 teaspoon chile garlic paste
8	ounces extra-firm tofu, cut into 1-inch cubes
1¼	cups brown rice or quinoa
1	large broccoli crown, cut into florets
1	green bell pepper, sliced
½	pound shiitake mushrooms, stems removed and caps sliced
1	large carrot, peeled and shredded

PREP + COOK TIME: 35 minutes

1. Preheat the oven or toaster oven to 425°F. Lightly coat a rimmed baking sheet with canola oil.

2. In a small bowl, combine ¼ cup of the tamari, the rice wine vinegar, honey, sesame oil, and garlic. Whisk and set aside.

3. In a large bowl, toss the tofu with 1 teaspoon of the canola oil and the remaining 1 tablespoon of the tamari. Transfer to the baking sheet and bake for 30 minutes, tossing halfway through.

4. Cook the brown rice or quinoa according to the package directions while the tofu bakes.

5. In a wide skillet, heat the remaining 1 tablespoon of canola oil over medium-high heat. Add the broccoli and bell pepper and sauté for 5 to 7 minutes, until just tender. Add the mushrooms and carrot and sauté for 5 minutes longer. Add the tamari mixture, cook 1 minute longer, then remove from the heat and set aside.

6. To serve, divide the rice evenly among 4 bowls. Top with the vegetables and tofu.

SERVES 4
PER SERVING: calories 265, fat 10 g, protein 12 g, carbohydrates 36 g, dietary fiber 5 g

franks-n-beans

You just might want to eat this cowboy-style meal in front of the campfire—but gathered 'round the kitchen table's OK, too. Serve up some gluten-free bread on the side to sop up the sweet sauce.

GLUTEN-FREE

DAIRY-FREE

NUT-FREE

EGG-FREE

ingredients

- 1 tablespoon canola oil
- 1 large yellow onion, diced
- 1 teaspoon smoked paprika
- ¾ cup tomato sauce
- 2 tablespoons molasses
- 3 tablespoons dark brown sugar
- 1 tablespoon wheat-free tamari
- 1 (15-ounce) can pinto beans, rinsed and drained
- 4 all-natural gluten-free hot dogs or veggie dogs, cut into 1-inch pieces

  Salt and freshly ground black pepper

SERVES 4

PER SERVING: calories 458, fat 20 g, protein 16 g, carbohydrates 57 g, dietary fiber 11 g

PREP TIME: 5 minutes
COOK TIME: 20 minutes

1. In a large skillet, heat the oil over medium heat. Add the onion and sauté for 5 to 7 minutes, until soft and translucent. Add the paprika and sauté for 30 seconds longer.

2. Add the tomato sauce, molasses, brown sugar, and tamari and cook for 1 to 2 minutes, until the mixture begins to bubble.

3. Add the pinto beans and hot dog pieces, and lower the heat to a simmer. Cook, partially covered, for 10 minutes, or until the pinto beans and hot dog pieces are warmed through and the flavors have blended. Season to taste with salt and pepper, and serve.

corn chip–crusted tofu fingers

Making this kid-meal staple with tofu means your meal has a smaller carbon footprint—but a just-as-big taste. If you'd prefer to bake these instead of fry, do so at 400°F for 30 minutes, or until the chip coating is golden-brown.

ingredients

½ **cup cornstarch**

½ **teaspoon salt**

2 **large eggs**

¾ **cup corn tortilla chips, finely crushed**

½ **cup grated Parmesan cheese**

1 **teaspoon dried basil**

½ **teaspoon dried thyme**

½ **teaspoon dried oregano**

¼ **teaspoon dried sage**

1 **pound extra-firm tofu, drained and patted dry, and sliced into 8 equal pieces**

2 **tablespoons canola oil**

Mighty Marinara Sauce, for dipping (page 56)

SERVES 4

PER SERVING: calories 432, fat 25 g, protein 22 g, carbohydrates 21 g, dietary fiber 2 g

PREP TIME: 15 to 20 minutes
COOK TIME: 10 to 12 minutes

1. Set out three medium bowls.

2. In the first bowl, add the cornstarch and salt. Crack the eggs into the second bowl and gently whisk. In the third bowl, add the corn chips, Parmesan cheese, basil, thyme, oregano, and sage and mix well.

3. Dredge each tofu finger in the cornstarch, then the eggs, and finally the corn chip mixture. Set aside on a plate.

4. Heat the canola oil in a large skillet over medium-high heat. Place each tofu finger flat in the pan. Cook for 3 to 4 minutes, then flip and cook for 2 to 3 minutes longer, until both sides are crispy. Remove from the pan and place on a paper towel to drain. Serve hot with the sauce.

COOKING WITH KIDS

teach your child to bread with two hands (less mess!)

STEP 1   Once your three bowls (filled with cornstarch, eggs, and corn chips) are set up in front of you, explain to your child that to get a crunchy coating to stick to a food, you need to create a "glue" with the cornstarch and eggs.

STEP 2   Have your child pick up a piece of tofu with her right hand and drop it in the cornstarch. Turn it over and spin it around until it looks good and floury.

STEP 3   Tell your child to pick up the tofu with her left hand and place it in the egg mixture. Wriggle the tofu around so it gets covered in egg.

STEP 4   With her left hand, your child can lift the tofu out of the egg mixture and drop it in the corn chip mixture. Then, using her right hand, she can toss it to coat.

STEP 5   Drop the coated tofu on a plate or rimmed baking sheet, and start over with a new piece. Remind your child which hands to use, so the cornstarch and egg glue stay on the tofu fingers—instead of on her fingers!

cool zucchini noodles

When it's too hot to cook, these zucchini "noodles" make a quick, nutritious meal. The sunflower seed and nutritional yeast topping add palate-pleasing nuttiness and crunch.

ingredients

½ **cup toasted sunflower seeds**

2 **tablespoons nutritional yeast**

 Salt and freshly ground black pepper

4 **large zucchini, peeled and ends trimmed**

1 **cup Mighty Marinara Sauce (page 56), cooled**

SERVES 4

PER SERVING: calories 151, fat 8 g, protein 7 g, carbohydrates 16 g, dietary fiber 6 g

PREP TIME: 10 minutes

1. In a food processor, add the sunflower seeds and nutritional yeast, and season with salt and pepper. Process until the sunflower seeds are the consistency of crumbs. Set aside.

2. Set out four plates or bowls. With a mandoline or vegetable peeler, shred the zucchini into thin strands, arranging one shredded zucchini on each plate or bowl.

3. Top each plate with ¼ cup of the marinara sauce and 2 to 3 tablespoons of the sunflower seed mixture. Serve at room temperature.

sweet potato gnocchi with lentils

Quick weeknight recipe this is not—but this cozy, stick-to-your ribs dish is well worth the effort when you have some time to spend in the kitchen. Toss a few large handfuls of spinach in with the red onion for some added nutrition.

DAIRY-FREE

NUT-FREE OPTION

EGG-FREE

SOY-FREE

ingredients

- 1 **cup French lentils, picked over and rinsed**
- 2 **pounds sweet potatoes, peeled and cut into 2-inch pieces**
- 1½ **cups whole-wheat pastry flour, plus more as needed**
- 1 **teaspoon salt, plus more as needed**
- ¼ **cup olive oil**
- 1 **medium red onion, sliced**
- 3 **cloves garlic, minced**
- ½ **cup walnuts, finely chopped (optional)**

PREP + COOK TIME: 75 minutes

1. Bring a large pot of water to a boil. Set out a rimmed baking sheet.

2. In a medium saucepan, add the lentils and enough water to cover by 2 to 3 inches. Cover, bring to a boil, then simmer, partially covered, for 20 to 25 minutes, until tender.

3. Add the sweet potatoes to the large pot and cook for 12 to 15 minutes, until easily pierced with a fork. Drain, rinse under cold water, and set aside until cool enough to touch.

4. In a large bowl, mash the sweet potatoes. Add the flour, ½ cup at a time, mixing to fully incorporate. The mixture should feel slightly sticky, but as if it will hold its shape when rolled into a thin rope. Add the salt and mix again.

5. On a floured surface, work in batches to roll the gnocchi dough into long ropes, about ½ inch thick. Slice each rope into ½-inch pieces, then use the back of a fork to make an indentation on the surface of each gnocchi. Transfer the gnocchi to the baking sheet and refrigerate while you prepare the remaining ingredients.

6. Bring a large pot of fresh water to a boil.

7. Heat the olive oil in a large skillet over medium-high heat. Add the onion and sauté for 5 to 7 minutes, until soft. Add the garlic and sauté for 1 minute longer. Add the lentils, walnuts, if using, and salt to taste and cook for 2 to 3 minutes, until heated through. Turn off the heat.

8. Add the gnocchi to the boiling water and cook for 1 to 2 minutes, until they begin to float near the surface. Drain, transfer to a large bowl, then add the lentil mixture and toss gently to combine. Serve immediately.

SERVES 8
PER SERVING: calories 296, fat 12 g, protein 7 g, carbohydrates 41 g, dietary fiber 8 g

teach your child to shape gnocchi

STEP 1 After making the gnocchi dough, have your child place a tennis ball–size piece of the mixture onto a floured surface. Using both palms, he can gently roll the dough back and forth, making it longer and thinner.

STEP 2 Once the dough is rolled into a rope about the thickness of two of your child's fingers (one grown-up finger), he can use a butter knife to cut the rope into individual gnocchi. Each gnocchi should be about as long as his thumb (about half a grown-up thumb).

STEP 3 Give your child a small fork. Have him use the back of the fork to make small indentations on the top of each gnocchi. This will help the gnocchi hold onto more of the sauce.

STEP 4 Repeat with the remaining dough. Now, the gnocchi are ready to cook!

mac-n-cheeze

Trying to replace the real taste and texture of cheese is no easy feat, but the creamy, cheese-like sauce in this kid staple is a welcome addition to dairy-free diets. If you'd like, add up to a cup of steamed veggies, like broccoli florets or chopped carrots, to the macaroni.

ingredients

Canola oil for coating the pan

¼ cup soy-free, nonhydrogenated margarine

¼ cup whole-wheat pastry flour

3 cups unsweetened rice milk

1½ cups nutritional yeast

2 tablespoons tahini

1 teaspoon salt

2 teaspoons umeboshi plum vinegar

8 ounces whole-wheat elbow macaroni

¼ cup panko bread crumbs

SERVES 8

PER SERVING: calories 328, fat 10 g, protein 17 g, carbohydrates 47 g, dietary fiber 9 g

PREP TIME: 20 minutes
COOK TIME: 25 minutes

1. Preheat the oven to 425°F. Lightly coat an 8-inch square baking pan with canola oil. Bring a large pot of water to a boil.

2. Meanwhile, in a medium saucepan, melt the margarine over medium heat. Whisk in the flour and cook for 1 minute, or until fragrant and lightly browned, then slowly whisk in the rice milk. Add the nutritional yeast, tahini, and salt and whisk well to combine. Simmer on low heat for 3 to 5 minutes, until slightly thickened, then remove from the heat, stir in the umeboshi vinegar, and return to a simmer, stirring occasionally for 5 to 7 minutes.

3. Cook the pasta in the boiling water, and drain when just slightly underdone.

4. Add the pasta to the baking pan and pour the cheese sauce mixture over the top. Stir gently to combine. Scatter the bread crumbs evenly over the top.

5. Bake for 12 to 15 minutes, until the bread crumbs are golden-brown. Serve with a green salad or steamed veggies.

greener sloppy joes

Where's the beef? Who cares! Lentils make for an equally tasty and protein-packed sand-wich filling that's easier on the planet (and your budget). If you've got any leftovers, try serving them over gluten-free elbow macaroni.

ingredients

- 1¼ **cups French lentils, picked over and rinsed**
- 1 **tablespoon olive oil**
- 1 **large yellow onion, diced**
- 2 **green bell peppers, diced**
- 2 **teaspoons ground cumin**
- 1 **teaspoon smoked paprika**
- 2 **tablespoons dark brown sugar**
- 1 **jalapeño pepper, seeded and minced (optional)**
- 2 **cups Mighty Marinara Sauce (page 56), or your favorite tomato sauce**
- ⅓ **cup water**
- **Salt**
- 6 **whole-wheat or gluten-free hamburger buns**

PREP + COOK TIME: 30 to 35 minutes

1. In a medium stockpot, add the lentils with enough water to cover by 2 to 3 inches. Cover, bring to a boil, then simmer, partially covered, for 20 to 25 minutes, until tender. Drain the lentils.

2. Meanwhile, in a large skillet, heat the olive oil over medium heat. Add the onion and sauté for 5 to 7 minutes, until soft and translucent. Add the bell peppers and sauté for 5 minutes longer.

3. Add the cumin, paprika, brown sugar, and jalapeño, if using. Cook for 1 minute, then add the marinara sauce and water. Season to taste with salt. Bring to a boil, then reduce to a simmer for 5 to 10 minutes.

4. Add the lentils to the sloppy joe mixture. Season to taste and cook for 5 minutes longer, until the flavors have blended.

5. Scoop the sloppy joe mixture into the hamburger buns and serve.

SERVES 6

PER SERVING: calories 300, fat 5 g, protein 11 g, carbohydrates 58 g, dietary fiber 9 g

lentil burgers

These are sort of like falafel, only bigger and even more delicious. Creamy avocado makes an ideal burger topping, but hummus or ketchup (or both) are equally delicious.

ingredients

1   tablespoon olive oil, plus more for coating the pan

1   cup French lentils, picked over and rinsed

1   medium yellow onion, diced

1   medium zucchini, coarsely shredded

⅓   cup brown rice flour

½   cup chopped fresh parsley

2   tablespoons tahini

2   teaspoons ground cumin

2   cloves garlic

Juice from ½ lemon

1½ teaspoons salt

8   whole-wheat or gluten-free hamburger buns

Sliced avocado, lettuce leaves, and tomato slices (optional)

PREP TIME: 35 minutes
BAKE TIME: 30 minutes

1. Preheat the oven to 425°F. Lightly coat a rimmed baking sheet with olive oil.

2. In a medium saucepan, add the lentils and enough water to cover by 2 to 3 inches. Cover, bring to a boil, and simmer for 25 minutes, until cooked.

3. While the lentils cook, prepare the vegetables. In a large skillet, heat the olive oil over medium heat. Add the onion and sauté for 5 to 7 minutes, until soft and translucent. Add the zucchini and sauté for 5 minutes longer. Remove from the heat and set aside.

4. In a food processor, add the lentils, onion, and zucchini. Process until nearly smooth. Add the brown rice flour, parsley, tahini, cumin, garlic, lemon juice, and salt and process until well-combined.

5. Form into eight ⅓-cup patties, putting them on the prepared baking sheet. Bake for 30 minutes, flipping halfway through. Serve in the burger buns with avocado, lettuce, and tomato, if using.

MAKES 8 BURGERS
PER BURGER (with bun): calories 250, fat 6 g, protein 10 g, carbohydrates 42 g, dietary fiber 7 g

olive oil
twice-baked potatoes

You don't need dairy to make rich, creamy mashed potatoes—and this recipe proves it! Nutritional yeast adds a kid-friendly, cheesy flavor, plus important B vitamins; find it at natural-food stores.

ingredients

2   **large russet potatoes, scrubbed and pierced with a fork several times**

2   **tablespoons olive oil**

2   **tablespoons unsweetened rice milk**

1   **tablespoon nutritional yeast**

¾   **teaspoon salt**

     Freshly ground black pepper

SERVES 4

PER SERVING: calories 268, fat 14 g, protein 5 g, carbohydrates 33 g, dietary fiber 5 g

PREP TIME: 15 minutes
BAKE TIME: 1 hour, 25 minutes

1. Preheat the oven to 400°F. Wrap the potatoes in foil, place on a rimmed baking sheet, and bake for 1 hour, or until easily pierced with a knife. Remove from the oven, slice in half lengthwise, and set aside for about 10 minutes, until cool enough to touch. Lower the oven temperature to 350°F.

2. Set out a medium bowl. Use a spoon to scoop the flesh out of the skins, taking care not to tear the skins, and place in the bowl.

3. Add the olive oil, rice milk, nutritional yeast, salt, and pepper to the potatoes and mash with a fork until well-combined. Adjust the salt and pepper to taste. Scoop the mixture evenly back into the 4 potato skins and transfer to the baking sheet.

4. Bake for 20 minutes, until hot, then broil on high for 5 minutes, until the tops of the potatoes are golden-brown. Serve with chicken, meat, fish, or tofu.

chicken potpie
with sweet potato topping

Who needs a boring old crust when you can have a dreamy, fluffy sweet potato topping? If you're pressed for time, use about 1½ cups of rotisserie chicken instead of roasting your own. This is also a great dish to double and freeze.

ingredients

PREP TIME: 35 minutes
COOK TIME: 30 to 40 minutes

SWEET POTATO TOPPING

1   **pound sweet potatoes, cut into 1-inch pieces (about 2½ cups)**

1   **tablespoon fresh lemon juice**

1   **large egg**

¼   **cup whole milk, or unsweetened almond milk, rice milk, or soymilk**

½   **teaspoon salt**

½   **teaspoon baking soda**

continued on page 96

1.   To make the sweet potato topping, bring a medium pot of salted water to a boil over high heat. Add the sweet potatoes to the boiling water, and cook for 10 to 12 minutes, until fork-tender.

2.   Drain the sweet potatoes, and add to a food processor. Add the lemon juice, egg, milk, salt, and baking soda. Puree for about 30 seconds, until smooth. Set aside.

3.   To make the filling, preheat the oven to 350°F. Bring a medium pot of salted water to a boil over high heat. Add the chicken cutlets, making certain the chicken pieces are completely submerged in the water.

4.   Cook the chicken for about 5 minutes, until done. Transfer the chicken to a large bowl, and let cool for 10 minutes. Cut into bite-size pieces.

5.   Meanwhile, in a large sauté pan or skillet, heat the canola oil over medium-high heat. Add the onion, and sauté, stirring, for about 5 minutes, until softened and translucent. Add the carrots and celery, cooking for 5 minutes longer, until mostly softened. Add the peas and stir to combine with the other vegetables, cooking for just 1 to 2 minutes, until warm. Season with salt and pepper to taste. Add the vegetables to the large bowl and mix with the reserved chicken pieces.

FILLING

¾ **pound chicken cutlets**

1 **tablespoon canola oil**

1 **cup chopped yellow onion (about 1 large onion)**

1 **cup diced carrots (about 2 medium carrots)**

1 **cup chopped celery (about 2 celery stalks)**

1½ **cups frozen peas, thawed**

Salt and freshly ground black pepper

2 **tablespoons butter or olive oil**

1 **cup chicken broth plus 1 cup whole milk, or unsweetened almond milk, rice milk, or soy milk; or 2 cups chicken broth**

2 **tablespoons cornstarch**

SERVES 4

PER SERVING: calories 431, fat 20 g, protein 33 g, carbohydrates 31 g, dietary fiber 6 g

6. Gently wipe the large sauté pan to reuse. Melt the butter or olive oil in the pan over medium-high heat, then add the broth, and season to taste with salt and pepper. Once the liquid begins to simmer, carefully transfer 4 tablespoons of hot liquid into a small bowl. Carefully stir the liquid with the cornstarch to make a slurry. Add the slurry back into the pan, whisking constantly to combine. Bring to a boil, still whisking, and cook for 1 to 2 minutes, until thickened enough to coat the back of a spoon. Remove from the heat.

7. Add the creamy sauce to the reserved vegetables and chicken. Mix to coat the vegetables and chicken with the sauce. Pour into a 9-inch pie plate. Spread an even layer of the reserved topping over the chicken and vegetables.

8. Bake the potpie for 30 to 40 minutes, until the sweet potato topping is puffy and brown on the edges. Let sit for 5 minutes and serve.

tuna–brown rice bake

This is not your grandmother's tuna casserole. Made with brown rice instead of noodles and packed with healthy fillers like edamame and soy cheese, this dish is still a kid-pleaser—but now it is also perfect for health-conscious parents.

ingredients

- 1 **tablespoon vegetable oil, plus more for coating the casserole dish**
- 1 **small yellow onion, chopped (about ½ cup)**
- ½ **cup chopped red bell pepper**
- 1 **clove garlic, minced**
- 3 **cups cooked brown rice**
- 1 **(10.75-ounce) can gluten-free cream of mushroom soup**
- 1 **(12-ounce) can water-packed tuna, drained**
- 1 **cup frozen shelled edamame or frozen peas**
- ½ **cup soymilk, milk, vegetable broth, or water**
- 1 **cup shredded cheddar soy cheese, or ½ cup grated Parmesan cheese combined with ½ cup shredded mozzarella cheese**
- ½ **teaspoon sea salt or salt**
- ¼ **teaspoon freshly ground black pepper**

PREP TIME: 15 minutes
COOK TIME: 30 minutes

1. Preheat the oven to 350°F. Coat a 2-quart casserole dish with vegetable oil or nonstick cooking spray.

2. Heat the vegetable oil in a large saucepan over medium heat until hot. Cook the onion and bell pepper for about 5 minutes, or until tender. Add the garlic and cook for 1 minute longer. Stir in the brown rice, soup, tuna, edamame or peas, soymilk, ½ cup of the cheese, and salt and pepper to taste. Cook and stir for 3 to 5 minutes, until well-combined.

3. Spoon the rice mixture into the prepared casserole dish. Bake, uncovered, for 25 minutes, until the rice is heated through. Remove from the oven and top with the remaining ½ cup of cheese. Return to the oven and bake for 5 minutes longer, or until the cheese is melted.

SERVES 6
PER SERVING: calories 510, fat 10 g, protein 24 g, carbohydrates 79 g, dietary fiber 5 g

beef satay with peanut noodles and snow peas

This recipe marinates skirt steak in pineapple juice, which contains bromelain, a natural enzyme that tenderizes meat. Just make sure not to marinate longer than a couple of hours or your meat will become too mushy.

ingredients

**PREP TIME: 25 minutes, plus
30 to 45 minutes to marinate the meat
COOK TIME: 10 minutes**

MEAT

1   **cup bottled pineapple juice**

¼   **cup canola oil**

1   **tablespoon freshly grated ginger**

2   **cloves garlic, minced**

   Salt

1½ **pounds flank steak, cut into 1-inch pieces**

6   **bamboo skewers**

1. In a medium-size flat dish, combine the pineapple juice, canola oil, ginger, garlic, and 1 teaspoon salt. Add the meat, cover, and let marinate at room temperature for 30 to 45 minutes.

2. Soak the skewers in cold water for 30 minutes.

3. Meanwhile, make the peanut sauce. In a food processor, add the peanut butter, ½ cup of roasted red peppers, sesame oil, honey, ginger, lime juice, ½ teaspoon of salt, and ¼ teaspoon of pepper. Puree for 30 seconds to 1 minute, until smooth. Remove ½ cup of the peanut sauce and reserve as a dipping sauce for the meat.

4. Preheat the broiler. Remove the meat from the marinade, and discard the marinade. Thread each piece lengthwise onto a skewer, dividing the meat evenly among the skewers. Arrange in a single layer on the baking sheet, then sprinkle the meat with salt and pepper.

SERVES 6

PER SERVING: calories 753, fat 46 g, protein 48 g, carbohydrates 40 g, dietary fiber 6 g

PEANUT SAUCE
AND NOODLES

1   **cup creamy peanut
    butter**

1½ **cups jarred sliced
    roasted red peppers**

3   **tablespoons sesame oil**

1   **tablespoon honey**

1   **tablespoon grated
    fresh ginger**

    Juice of 1 lime

    **Salt and freshly ground
    black pepper**

1   **(16-ounce) package
    thin rice noodles**

½   **pound snow peas,
    trimmed**

½   **cup chopped peanuts**

5. Bring a medium pot of salted water to a boil over high heat. Add the noodles, and after 2 minutes, add the snow peas. Cook for about 4 minutes total, until the noodles are al dente. Drain into a colander, then return to the pot and toss immediately with the peanut sauce. Stir in the remaining 1 cup roasted red pepper slices, and top with the peanuts. Cover and keep warm.

6. Broil the skewers on one baking sheet at a time, cooking for 2 minutes per side for medium-rare meat. Serve the meat warm or at room temperature with the reserved ½ cup of peanut sauce, along with the noodles and snow peas.

spicy mexican shrimp skewers

Surprise your guests at the next barbecue by serving shrimp alongside the usual fare. The Mexican sauce is super easy to make and is equally tasty on chicken and steak. To keep the wooden skewers from burning, soak in water for 15 minutes before using.

ingredients

16	**large shrimp, peeled and deveined**
1	**large mango, peeled, pitted, and cut into ½-inch chunks**
2	**tablespoons canola oil**
	Juice of 2 limes
1	**chipotle in adobo sauce, finely chopped**
½	**teaspoon freshly ground black pepper**
1	**clove garlic, minced**
¼	**cup finely chopped fresh cilantro**
	Brown rice, for serving

PREP TIME: 10 minutes
COOK TIME: 8 minutes

1. Preheat a gas or charcoal grill to medium.

2. In a large bowl, toss the shrimp and mango with the canola oil, lime juice, chipotle in adobo sauce, pepper, garlic, and cilantro.

3. Thread the shrimp and mango onto skewers, alternating shrimp with mango so that each skewer has 4 shrimp and 3 pieces of mango.

4. Place the skewers on the grill and cook for 4 minutes on each side, until the shrimp are pink and cooked through. Serve alongside brown rice.

SERVES 4
PER SKEWER: calories 86, fat 7 g, protein 5 g, carbohydrates 1 g, dietary fiber 0 g

cheesy stuffed pizza burgers

Combining two kid favorites—pizza and burgers—means you've got a recipe for success. Plus, turkey is a great choice for burgers because it's so lean, but you can create a juicier dish without as much fat as a beef burger just by adding a bit of canola oil.

PREP TIME: 10 minutes
COOK TIME: 15 minutes

ingredients

¼ cup finely chopped yellow onion

¼ cup chopped fresh Italian parsley

2 tablespoons tomato paste

1 tablespoon canola oil

1 teaspoon dried Italian seasoning

Sea salt and freshly ground black pepper

1½ pounds 93 percent lean ground turkey

3 ounces cheese, grated or crumbled, such as feta, Italian cheese blend, or Italian-style soy cheese

6 whole-wheat or gluten-free hamburger buns

Additional cheese, sliced olives, tomatoes, chopped fresh basil, lettuce, for serving (optional)

1. In a large bowl, stir together the onion, parsley, tomato paste, 1 teaspoon of the oil, and the Italian seasoning. Season to taste with salt and pepper. Add the turkey and mix well.

2. Divide the cheese into 6 portions. Divide the turkey mixture into 6 portions. Make an indentation, using your thumb, in each portion of the turkey mixture and insert one portion of cheese. Reshape the turkey mixture around the cheese, pinching to seal the cheese in the center. Flatten into patties.

3. Brush the remaining 2 teaspoons of canola oil on a grill heated to medium, or heat the oil in a large skillet over medium heat. Cook the burgers for about 15 minutes total, turning once, or until the internal temperature of the meat reaches 165°F.

4. Place each burger on a bun and serve with your family's favorite condiments, if using.

SERVES 6
PER SERVING: calories 430, fat 22 g, protein 36 g, carbohydrates 21 g, dietary fiber 3 g

easy lemon chicken

A quick prep time and a few simple ingredients make this dish a great go-to for busy nights. But the flavor is anything but ordinary: The roasted lemon infuses the chicken with flavor, and the lemon thyme gives it an extra boost of brightness, though regular thyme works well, too.

ingredients

- 2 **tablespoons canola oil**
- 2 **cloves garlic, pressed through a garlic press**
- 2 **teaspoons chopped fresh lemon thyme or regular thyme**
- 1½ **pounds chicken thighs and/or legs**
- 1 **pound new potatoes or baby Dutch yellow potatoes, halved**
- 1 **(12-ounce) bag baby carrots**
- 1 **lemon, cut into 4 wedges**
- ½ **teaspoon sea salt or kosher salt**
- ¼ **teaspoon freshly ground black pepper**

SERVES 4

PER SERVING: calories 497, fat 20 g, protein 52 g, carbohydrates 26 g, dietary fiber 5 g

PREP TIME: 10 minutes
COOK TIME: 45 minutes

1. Preheat the oven to 425°F. Combine the canola oil, garlic, and thyme in a small bowl. Arrange the chicken on one side of a 9 by 13-inch baking dish. Place the potatoes, carrots, and lemon wedges on the other side. Drizzle the chicken and vegetables with the oil mixture and toss to coat well.

2. Turn the chicken skin side up. Sprinkle the chicken and vegetables with salt and pepper.

3. Roast, uncovered, for 45 to 50 minutes, until the chicken's internal temperature reaches 165°F, stirring the vegetables and lemon wedges once or twice. Remove and cover the vegetables if they are tender and golden-brown before the chicken is fully cooked.

4. To serve, allow the lemon wedges to cool slightly, then squeeze over the chicken and vegetables.

all-day
roast pork shoulder

Not to worry: This dish just sounds like it takes forever to make, but really it requires only about 30 minutes of work. As you leave the roast to cook, your home will fill with a delicious ginger and brown sugar aroma you'll enjoy all day. Unless you invite another family or two over for dinner, you'll have a lot of leftovers: Shred it with a fork and add barbecue sauce for pulled-pork sandwiches.

ingredients

½   **teaspoon red pepper flakes**

½   **teaspoon freshly ground black pepper**

¼   **teaspoon ground anise**

2   **teaspoons ground cinnamon**

2   **cloves garlic, chopped**

1   **2-inch piece fresh ginger, grated**

¼   **cup Dijon mustard**

½   **cup packed brown sugar**

3   **tablespoons pure maple syrup**

3   **tablespoons wheat-free tamari**

½   **teaspoon salt**

1   **tablespoon extra-virgin olive oil**

1   **(6 to 8-pound) pork shoulder roast, rolled and tied**

PREP TIME: 30 minutes
COOK TIME: 8 to 12 hours

1.   In a small bowl, combine the pepper flakes, pepper, anise, and cinnamon. Set aside. In a small food processor, combine the ground spices with the garlic, ginger, mustard, brown sugar, maple syrup, tamari, salt, and olive oil. Blend to a fairly smooth paste, though a few chunks are fine.

2.   Rub the spice marinade all over the roast, getting into the nooks and crannies of the meat with your fingers. Allow to marinate at room temperature for 20 minutes.

3.   Meanwhile, preheat the oven to 450°F and place a rack in the middle. Make sure there is enough clearance to fit in your roast without hitting the top shelf or the top of the oven. Fit a roasting pan with a rack.

4.   Set the roast on the rack in the roasting pan, fat side up. Roast for 30 minutes.

5. Remove the roast from the oven, carefully flip it over, and return to the oven. Turn the temperature down to 225°F. Roast for 8 to 12 hours, flipping once in the middle of the cooking time. The longer you cook the roast, the more tender it will be—you can even cook it up to 12 hours, depending on the size.

6. Serve the pork with Mac-n-Cheeze (page 89) and a salad. Leftovers will keep in an airtight container for up to 5 days.

MAKES 20 (4-OUNCE) SERVINGS
PER SERVING: calories 430, fat 30 g, protein 32 g, carbohydrates 6 g, dietary fiber 0 g

healthy turkey stir-fry with broccoli and cashews

Ground turkey is an underappreciated meat in the stir-fry world, which is a shame because it cooks up tender and savory, lending its rich flavor to vegetables. Stir-fried with broccoli and crunchy cashews, the texture of this dish alone is worth writing home about; the fact that it's quick, easy, and perfect for a busy weeknight is a bonus.

ingredients

5	tablespoons olive oil
2	heads broccoli, cut into florets (about 4 cups)
1	large yellow onion, chopped
3	cloves garlic, minced
1	tablespoon water
2	pounds 93 percent lean ground turkey
3	zucchini, cut lengthwise, then into ½-inch half-circles
½	cup whole cashews
¼	cup wheat-free tamari
1	teaspoon freshly ground black pepper

SERVES 6

PER SERVING: calories 515, fat 32 g, protein 45 g, carbohydrates 11 g, dietary fiber 2 g

PREP + COOK TIME: 30 minutes

1. In a large saucepan, heat 2 tablespoons of the olive oil over medium heat. Add the broccoli and cook, uncovered, stirring occasionally, for 20 minutes. You want the broccoli to brown, but not burn. While the broccoli is cooking, work on step 2.

2. Heat 2 tablespoons of the olive oil in a smaller saucepan over low heat. Add the chopped onion and cook, stirring occasionally to keep it from burning, for about 12 minutes, or until it begins to caramelize and smell sweet. Add the garlic and about 1 tablespoon of water, and stir constantly for 2 minutes. Then add the ground turkey and use a spatula to break up the larger chunks. Turn up the heat to medium and cook, stirring occasionally to keep the onion and garlic from burning, for about 20 minutes, or until turkey is cooked through. Remove from the heat and set aside.

3. Add the zucchini and the remaining 1 tablespoon of olive oil to the cooking broccoli. Cook, stirring occasionally, for 5 minutes. Allow the zucchini to brown and blister a bit, but don't let it burn. Add the cashews and cook for 7 minutes longer, until they darken in color, stirring occasionally.

4. Add the cooked turkey to the vegetables, stir well, and cook for 2 minutes. Add the tamari and pepper, stir well again, and cook for 3 minutes longer. Serve hot.

recycle your food!
five ideas for leftovers

Chew on this: Nearly 40 percent of the food in the United States goes right into the trash. What's more, that number has risen by half since 1974, according to the National Institutes of Health. Instead of letting leftovers linger too long in the fridge—then tossing them in the garbage—consider these ideas for five brand new meals.

IF YOU HAVE THIS	MAKE THIS	HERE'S HOW
Pasta (wheat or gluten-free)	Pasta frittata	Combine leftover **noodles** with 6 beaten eggs. Flavor with herbs, grated cheese, or leftover veggies, and bake until set.
Cooked vegetables	Veggie pockets	Prepare Gluten-Free Pizza Dough (page 48) or your favorite pizza dough. Divide the dough into 4 equal pieces and roll into circles, ⅛ to ¼ inch thick. Place leftover **veggies** on one side and fold the empty side of the dough over the top, crimping to seal. Bake until the crust is golden-brown.
Roast or grilled chicken	White chicken chili	Combine shredded **chicken** with sautéed onions and garlic, white beans, chili powder, and canned green chile peppers. Add enough broth to cover and simmer, until the flavors are well-blended. Top with grated Jack cheese, if desired.
Mashed potatoes	Potato-stuffed peppers	Combine mashed **potatoes** with cooked veggies of your choice (peas and carrots are tasty). Scoop into seeded bell peppers and bake until the peppers have softened and the mashed potatoes are golden.
Meatballs	Meat lasagne	Use your fingers or a food processor to crumble the **meatballs** into coarse crumbles. Use as a filling in your favorite lasagne recipe.

dessert

WHAT'S DESSERT doing in a healthy-food cookbook? It proves that you can have a nutritious, balanced diet that includes sweets—if you want to.

Plenty of parents feel strongly about keeping refined sugar out of their kitchens—and their kids' mouths—as long as possible. If that's you, there are a few great recipes in this chapter that are free of straight sugar, from fruit-filled ice pops to almond honey cakes. Others call for raw cane sugar (to help you avoid the overprocessed stuff), molasses, or other natural sources of sweetness. We've also combined sugar with some healthy ingredients like fruit and flaxseed. Not always, though: Sometimes dessert is just dessert (but allergy-friendly, of course).

If you're a family that loves your sweets, then you already know the trick is moderation. That's why it's doubly important to make delicious recipes. Who wants to serve up sugar and calories if they aren't going to thrill the taste buds? The healthy approach to dessert is about being mindful of eating—enjoying every last bite of that gluten-free pie or dairy-free hot cocoa, instead of grabbing a processed piece of candy every time you walk by the kitchen. Kids with allergies are already old hands at watching out for what's okay to eat and what isn't—so letting them indulge in sweets they *can* eat is, well, like icing on the cake.

Chocolate Toasties G option, D, N, E, S 111

Coconut No-Cream Pie G option, D, N, E 113

Chocolate Crumb Crust G option, D, N, E, S 114

Butternut Blondies D, N, E, S 116

Sunset Pops G, D, N, E, S 117

Cherry Chocolate Sorbet G, D, N, E, S 119

Cozy Baked Apples G, D, N, E, S 120

Mixed-Berry Fool G, N, E, S 121

Nutty Fruit Pizza G, D, S 122

Ginger Chip Drop Cookies G, D, N, E, S 124

No Moo Chocolate Pudding G, D, N, E 127

Raspberry Oat Bars G, D, N, E, S 129

Whole-Wheat Lemon Shortbread D, N, E, S 130

The World's Simplest Soft Serve G, D, N, E, S 131

Salted Caramel Hot Cocoa G, D, N, E 132

Raw Summer Peach Tart G, D, E, S 134

Almost-Raw Chocolate Cashew Fudge G, D, S 137

Almond Flour Honey Cakes G, D option, S option 138

Gluten-Free Pie Crust G, D, N, E, S 139

Spiced Pumpkin Pie G, D, N, E 140

chocolate toasties

Chocolate-filled sandwiches with cinnamon and sugar? An unconventional dessert, for sure, but one that's quick to put together and a soon-to-be family favorite.

ingredients

½ **cup raw cane sugar**

1 **tablespoon ground cinnamon**

½ **cup sunflower seed butter**

¼ **cup unsweetened rice milk**

2 **tablespoons unsweetened cocoa powder**

½ **teaspoon vanilla extract**

Pinch of salt

8 **slices whole-wheat or gluten-free bread, crusts removed**

¼ **cup soy-free, nonhydrogenated margarine**

SERVES 8

PER SERVING: calories 323, fat 16 g, protein 7 g, carbohydrates 41 g, dietary fiber 3 g

PREP TIME: 10 minutes
COOK TIME: 10 minutes

1. In a shallow dish, combine ¼ cup of the sugar and the cinnamon. Set aside.

2. In a food processor, add the sunflower seed butter, rice milk, the remaining ¼ cup sugar, the cocoa powder, vanilla, and salt. Process until smooth.

3. Spread the sunflower seed butter mixture equally on each of four slices of the bread, then top with the remaining four slices of bread to make four sandwiches.

4. Melt 2 tablespoons of the margarine in a wide skillet over medium-high heat. Use a pastry brush to brush the melted margarine on both sides of each sandwich. Dip both sides of each sandwich in the cinnamon sugar mixture.

5. Melt the remaining 2 tablespoons of margarine in the skillet, and toast two sandwiches at a time, for 1 to 2 minutes on each side.

6. Slice each sandwich in half and serve immediately.

coconut
no-cream pie

Who needs milk or eggs to make a creamy, custardy dessert? Not you! Since most of the richness comes from the coconut milk, use a full-fat variety—it's worth it.

ingredients

PREP TIME: 5 minutes
BAKE + CHILL TIME: 4 hours

1	**Chocolate Crumb Crust (page 114)**
1	**(12-ounce) package firm silken tofu, drained**
1	**(14-ounce) can coconut milk**
¾	**cup raw cane sugar**
⅓	**cup cornstarch**
½	**teaspoon vanilla extract**
¼	**teaspoon almond extract**
¼	**teaspoon salt**
⅛	**teaspoon ground nutmeg**
1	**cup unsweetened shredded coconut**
½	**cup unsweetened large flake coconut**

1. Preheat the oven to 350°F. Set out the Chocolate Crumb Crust.

2. In a food processor, add the silken tofu and coconut milk and process until smooth. Add the sugar, cornstarch, vanilla, almond extract, salt, and nutmeg and process again until combined.

3. Pour the mixture into a large bowl. Add the shredded coconut and stir to combine.

4. Pour the mixture into the prepared pie crust and bake for 30 minutes, or until lightly browned on top. Top with the large flake coconut, and bake for 10 to 15 minutes longer, until the coconut flakes are toasted.

5. Allow the pie to chill in the refrigerator for at least 3 hours before serving.

SERVES 8

PER SERVING: calories 366, fat 22 g, protein 5 g, carbohydrates 38 g, dietary fiber 2 g

chocolate crumb crust

This crunchy, crumbly crust tastes especially delicious with a coconut filling, but you can't go wrong using it for peanut butter or ice cream pies, too.

ingredients

¼ **cup soy-free, nonhydrogenated margarine, melted, plus more for coating pie plate**

7½ **ounces chocolate graham crackers or wafer cookies, or gluten-free chocolate cookies**

PREP TIME: 5 minutes
BAKE TIME: 10 minutes

1. Preheat the oven to 350°F. Lightly coat a 9-inch pie plate with margarine.

2. In a food processor, add the chocolate cookies and process until finely pulverized. Add the melted margarine and process until well-combined.

3. Pat the mixture evenly into the pie plate. Bake for 10 minutes. Allow to cool before filling.

MAKES 1 PIE CRUST, SERVES 8
PER SERVING: calories 132, fat 8 g, protein 2 g, carbohydrates 15 g, dietary fiber 1 g

teach your child to shape a cookie-crumb crust

STEP 1 Once the cookies and margarine have been turned into crumbs by the food processor, remove the processor blade and help your child slowly dump the crumbs into the bottom of a 9-inch pie plate.

STEP 2 Give your child a ¼-cup measuring cup, and show her how to press down on the crumbs so that they stick together and form a layer about ¼ inch thick. Start from the middle and work your way to the edges.

STEP 3 When she gets near the sides, show her how to use the side of the measuring cup to press the crumbs up the side of the dish.

STEP 4 To make a smooth, even edge along the top rim of the crust, older kids can build the side of the crust and use their fingers to press down along the top at the same time. For younger kids who can't do both at once, work together: She builds the side while you press down on the top. Now it's ready to bake!

butternut blondies

Blondies will probably never be a health food, but that doesn't mean you can't sneak in a few better-for-you ingredients. This vegan version is loaded with fiber, thanks to whole-wheat pastry flour and ground flaxseed. Vitamin A comes from the butternut squash, which also lends extra moisture and sweetness.

DAIRY-FREE

NUT-FREE

EGG-FREE

SOY-FREE

ingredients

Canola oil, for coating the baking pan

¾ **cup soy-free, nonhydrogenated margarine, melted**

1½ **cups packed dark brown sugar**

2 **tablespoons ground flaxseed whisked with ¼ cup warm water**

1 **teaspoon vanilla extract**

½ **cup butternut squash puree**

1½ **cups whole-wheat pastry flour**

1½ **teaspoons baking powder**

1½ **teaspoons ground cinnamon**

½ **teaspoon salt**

¼ **teaspoon ground nutmeg**

½ **cup gluten-free, dairy-free, soy-free chocolate chips**

PREP TIME: 10 minutes
BAKE TIME: 20 to 25 minutes

1. Preheat the oven to 350°F. Coat an 8-inch square baking pan with canola oil.

2. In a large bowl, add the melted margarine and brown sugar and mix well. Add the flaxseed mixture and vanilla and stir to combine. Add the squash puree and stir again, until all the ingredients are incorporated.

3. Add the whole-wheat pastry flour, baking powder, cinnamon, salt, and nutmeg to the squash mixture and stir gently to combine. Fold in the chocolate chips.

4. Pour the batter into the prepared pan and bake for 20 to 25 minutes, until lightly browned at the edges.

5. Set aside to cool completely, then cut into 16 squares. Store in an airtight container for up to 2 days.

MAKES 16 BLONDIES
PER BLONDIE: calories 202, fat 9 g, protein 2 g, carbohydrates 37 g, dietary fiber 2 g

sunset pops

When the dog days of summer hit, cool off the kids with these tangy, fruit-filled treats. They're free of added sugar, so you can feel good about serving Sunset Pops as snacks, too.

ingredients

2   **cups frozen raspberries, slightly thawed**

1   **cup pure apple juice**

2   **cups frozen diced pineapple, slightly thawed**

8   **(3.5-ounce) paper cups or frozen-treat molds**

8   **treat sticks**

MAKES 8 POPS

PER POP: calories 48, fat 0 g, protein 0 g, carbohydrates 12 g, dietary fiber 3 g

PREP TIME: 10 minutes
CHILL TIME: 3 to 4 hours

1.   In a food processor, add the raspberries and ½ cup of the apple juice and process until smooth (strain to remove the raspberry seeds, if you'd like). Transfer the mixture to a bowl and set aside.

2.   Add the pineapple and the remaining ½ cup of the apple juice to the food processor. Process until completely smooth and transfer to another bowl.

3.   Spoon the raspberry mixture evenly into the 8 cups, so each cup is about halfway full. Spoon the pineapple mixture evenly into the 8 cups on top of the raspberry mixture, so each cup is nearly full. Don't worry, both mixtures are so thick the two won't mix together.

4.   Place a small piece of parchment paper over the surface of each cup. Stick a treat stick through the parchment paper and the center of each cup; the parchment will keep the stick in place while the pops freeze.

5.   Freeze for 3 to 4 hours, until the pops are completely frozen. Peel off the paper cup and parchment paper before serving.

cherry chocolate sorbet

I scream, you scream, we all scream for . . . sorbet! Rich cocoa powder plus a splash of rice milk make this fruity treat taste more like ice cream than sorbet, but it's entirely dairy-free.

ingredients

- 2 **cups frozen pitted cherries**
- **2 to 3 tablespoons unsweetened rice milk**
- 2 **tablespoons unsweetened cocoa powder**
- 2 **tablespoons gluten-free, dairy-free, soy-free chocolate chips**
- 1 **teaspoon honey (optional)**

SERVES 4

PER SERVING: calories 90, fat 3 g, protein 1 g, carbohydrates 18 g, dietary fiber 3 g

PREP TIME: 5 minutes

1. In a food processor, add the cherries and 2 tablespoons of the rice milk and process for 1 to 2 minutes, until well-combined. If the mixture seems dry, add the remaining 1 tablespoon rice milk.

2. Add the cocoa powder, chocolate chips, and honey, if using, and process again until well-combined. Serve immediately.

cozy
baked apples

Nothing says fall like homey baked apples. Enjoy this crumble-topped treat warm with a scoop of coconut milk–based ice cream, or even as a breakfast treat (hey, it does have fruit!) with a dollop of nondairy yogurt. Please note that this recipe calls for potato starch, not potato flour.

ingredients

Canola oil, for coating the baking dish

½ **cup gluten-free rolled oats**

½ **cup sorghum flour**

2 **tablespoons potato starch**

2 **tablespoons tapioca starch**

½ **cup packed dark brown sugar**

½ **teaspoon salt**

¼ **cup soy-free, nonhydrogenated margarine, cut into small pieces**

4 **Granny Smith apples, peeled and sliced into ½-inch pieces**

2 **tablespoons raw cane sugar**

1 **tablespoon cornstarch**

1 **tablespoon ground cinnamon**

1 **teaspoon ground ginger**

Juice of ½ small lemon

¼ **cup raisins (optional)**

PREP TIME: 10 minutes
BAKE TIME: 40 minutes

1. Preheat the oven to 350°F. Lightly coat an 8-inch square baking dish with canola oil.

2. In a medium bowl, add the oats, sorghum flour, potato starch, tapioca starch, brown sugar, and ¼ teaspoon of the salt, and mix well with a fork. Add the margarine and use your fingers or a fork to combine it with the flour mixture, forming coarse crumbs. Set aside.

3. In a large bowl, add the apple slices, sugar, cornstarch, cinnamon, ginger, the remaining ¼ teaspoon salt, the lemon juice, and raisins, if using. Toss well to combine.

4. Pour the apple mixture into the baking pan in an even layer. Top evenly with the oat mixture.

5. Bake for 40 minutes, or until the apples have softened and the oat mixture is lightly browned. Serve hot, cold, or at room temperature.

SERVES 8
PER SERVING: calories 260, fat 7 g, protein 2 g, carbohydrates 59 g, dietary fiber 5 g

mixed-berry fool

GLUTEN-FREE

NUT-FREE

EGG-FREE

SOY-FREE

This dessert "fools" you into thinking you're eating a hard-to-prepare mousse, but the truth is much simpler. You can have this decadent dessert on the table in just 20 minutes.

ingredients

1 **pint mixed berries, hulled and sliced**

4 **tablespoons raw cane sugar**

1 **cup heavy cream**

1 **teaspoon vanilla extract**

PREP TIME: 20 minutes

1. Combine the berries with 2 tablespoons of the sugar in a medium bowl and set aside for 10 minutes to allow the berries to release their juices. Using your hands, crush the berries so that only small pieces remain.

2. Combine the cream with the remaining 2 tablespoons of sugar and the vanilla in a stand mixer fitted with a whisk. Mix on medium-high speed until the cream is stiff and holds peaks easily, about 1 minute. Gently fold the cream into the berries in two batches. Serve immediately, or refrigerate for up to 2 hours.

SERVES 6

PER SERVING: calories 127, fat 7 g, protein 0 g, carbohydrates 15 g, dietary fiber 2 g

nutty fruit pizza

A buttery almond crust strikes the perfect balance with sweet strawberry, kiwifruit, and blueberry. Plus, it's superfun to eat. You can use whatever jam and fruits are your family's favorites: Have your kids get creative!

ingredients

- 1 **tablespoon canola oil, plus more for coating the pan**
- 2 **cups almond flour**
- 3 **tablespoons raw cane sugar**
- ⅛ **teaspoon salt**
- 1 **large egg, lightly beaten**
- ½ **teaspoon almond extract**
- ⅔ **cup natural strawberry jam**
- 1 **kiwifruit, sliced into six rounds**
- ¼ **cup blueberries**

PREP TIME: 20 minutes
BAKE TIME: 15 minutes

1. Preheat the oven to 350°F. Lightly coat a 9-inch round springform pan with canola oil.

2. In a large bowl, add the almond flour, sugar, and salt and mix with a fork. Add the egg, canola oil, and almond extract and mix to combine completely.

3. Use a spatula to press the dough into the bottom of the springform pan. Bake for 15 to 17 minutes, until the edges are golden-brown. Set aside to cool completely.

4. Pop the base out of the springform pan. Use a spatula to spread the jam evenly across the almond flour crust, leaving a ¼ to ½-inch border.

5. Arrange the kiwifruit slices in a circle around the edge of the jam, and arrange the blueberries in the center. Serve.

SERVES 10

PER SERVING: calories 193, fat 12 g, protein 5 g, carbohydrates 19 g, dietary fiber 3 g

ginger chip drop cookies

The classic chocolate chip cookie gets spiced up with a kick of ginger in this delicious gluten-free version. Dunk in a glass of your favorite nondairy milk for a seriously satisfying sweet. Please note that this recipe calls for potato starch, not potato flour.

ingredients

Canola oil, for coating the pan

1   **cup sorghum flour**

¼   **cup tapioca flour**

¼   **cup potato starch**

1   **tablespoon ground ginger**

1   **teaspoon baking powder**

½   **teaspoon salt**

¾   **teaspoon xanthan gum**

½   **cup soy-free, nonhydrogenated margarine, at room temperature**

PREP TIME: 5 minutes
BAKE TIME: 12 to 14 minutes

1.   Preheat the oven to 350°F. Coat two baking sheets with canola oil.

2.   In a medium bowl, add the sorghum flour, tapioca flour, potato starch, ginger, baking powder, salt, and xanthan gum. Mix well to combine.

3.   In a bowl or stand mixer, beat the margarine for about 30 seconds, until creamy. Add the brown sugar and cane sugar and beat again for 1 to 2 minutes, until light and fluffy. Add the molasses, flaxseed mixture, and vanilla, mixing well to combine.

4.   Slowly add the dry ingredients to the wet, mixing well to combine. Fold in the chocolate chips.

½ **cup packed dark brown sugar**

¼ **cup raw cane sugar**

2 **tablespoons molasses**

1 **tablespoon ground flaxseed whisked with 2 tablespoons warm water**

1 **teaspoon vanilla extract**

½ **cup gluten-free, dairy-free, soy-free chocolate chips**

5. Use a tablespoon to drop the dough onto the baking sheets. Bake for 12 to 14 minutes, until the cookies are just beginning to brown around the edges.

6. Let the cookies cool on the baking sheets for 3 to 5 minutes, then transfer to a wire rack and allow to cool completely.

MAKES ABOUT 20 COOKIES

PER COOKIE: calories 142, fat 7 g, protein 1 g, carbohydrates 24 g, dietary fiber 1 g

COOKING WITH KIDS

teach your child
to melt chocolate

STEP 1   Help your child make a double boiler. Have him fill a small saucepan about one-third of the way with water, then place a heatproof bowl on top.

STEP 2   While you place the double boiler on the stove over medium-low heat, he can measure out the amount of chocolate that needs to be melted. Help him pour the chocolate into the bowl.

STEP 3   Wearing oven mitts, help your child stir the chocolate with a spatula or wooden spoon. Slowly, the chocolate will begin to melt as the water in the saucepan gets warmer.

STEP 4   Once the chocolate has fully melted, help your child remove the bowl from the saucepan. Now he can use the melted chocolate for his recipe!

no moo
chocolate pudding

You probably won't find a simpler pudding recipe than this one—or a tastier one. Need proof? It's in the pudding. Serve alone, with fruit for dipping, or use as a filling for chocolate pie.

ingredients

1   **(12-ounce) package soft silken tofu**

½   **teaspoon vanilla extract**

¾   **cup gluten-free, dairy-free, soy-free chocolate chips**

PREP TIME: 5 minutes
CHILL TIME: 1 hour

1. Place the tofu and vanilla in a food processor and process until smooth.

2. Melt the chocolate in a double boiler over medium-low heat. Allow the chocolate to cool slightly, then add to the tofu mixture. Process again until smooth.

3. Transfer the pudding to a medium bowl or four small cups and refrigerate for at least 1 hour before serving.

SERVES 4
PER SERVING: calories 256, fat 16 g, protein 4 g, carbohydrates 30 g, dietary fiber 3 g

**I-CAN'T-BELIEVE-IT'S-NOT-BUTTERCREAM
CHOCOLATE CAKE, PAGE 185**

Berry Bars

raspberry oat bars

Wholesome and sweet, these gluten-free squares are a healthy hit with kids and adults alike. If your family prefers a different flavor of jam, swap the raspberry out for strawberry, blueberry, or fig. Please note that this recipe calls for potato starch, not potato flour.

ingredients

Canola oil, for coating the pan

1 cup sorghum flour

¼ cup tapioca flour

¼ cup potato starch

¾ teaspoon xanthan gum

½ teaspoon salt

¾ cup soy-free, nonhydrogenated margarine

¾ cup packed brown sugar

1 teaspoon vanilla extract

1 cup gluten-free oats

1 cup all-natural raspberry jam

MAKES 16 BARS

PER BAR: calories 184, fat 10 g, protein 2 g, carbohydrates 27 g, dietary fiber 2 g

PREP TIME: 5 to 10 minutes
BAKE TIME: 20 to 25 minutes

1. Preheat the oven to 350°F. Coat an 8-inch square baking pan with canola oil.

2. In a food processor, add the sorghum flour, tapioca flour, potato starch, xanthan gum, salt, margarine, brown sugar, and vanilla. Pulse to process until just combined.

3. Transfer the dough to a bowl and use a mixer (or your hands) to mix in the oats.

4. Divide the dough in half. Press half of the dough into the bottom of the prepared baking pan. With a spatula, spread the raspberry jam on top. Scatter the remaining dough in small clumps across the top of the jam.

5. Bake for 20 to 25 minutes, until the top is lightly browned. Allow to cool completely before slicing. The bars will keep in an airtight container for up to 2 days.

whole-wheat lemon shortbread

Add some zip to basic shortbread cookies with nutty whole wheat and bright lemon zest. Or you can substitute some equally delicious orange or lime zest if you prefer.

DAIRY-FREE

NUT-FREE

EGG-FREE

SOY-FREE

ingredients

Canola oil, for coating the pan

1 cup soy-free, nonhydrogenated margarine, at room temperature

½ cup raw cane sugar

1 teaspoon finely grated lemon zest

½ teaspoon vanilla extract

½ teaspoon salt

1½ cups whole-wheat pastry flour

1 tablespoon turbinado sugar

MAKES 12 PIECES
PER PIECE: calories 228, fat 16 g, protein 2 g, carbohydrates 21 g, dietary fiber 2 g

PREP TIME: 10 minutes
BAKE TIME: 22 minutes

1. Preheat the oven to 350°F. Lightly coat a 9-inch round cake pan with canola oil.

2. In a large bowl or stand mixer, beat the margarine for about 2 minutes, until creamy. Add the cane sugar and beat for 2 minutes longer, or until light and fluffy. Add the lemon zest, vanilla, and salt and beat until combined.

3. In ½-cup increments, add the flour and mix until thoroughly combined.

4. Transfer the dough to the cake pan, using a spatula to spread evenly; it may look like you won't have enough dough, but you will. Sprinkle the top evenly with the turbinado sugar.

5. Bake for 20 to 22 minutes, until the edges are lightly browned. Cool completely before slicing into 12 wedges.

the world's simplest soft serve

You might not expect it, but pureed frozen bananas make for a deliciously creamy dessert that's dairy-free and packed with nutrition. The frozen banana pieces will first appear crumbly in the food processor—but after a minute, they'll whip up into the texture of soft serve ice cream.

ingredients

4   large frozen bananas, cut into large chunks

Optional add-ins:

- **ground cinnamon or ginger**
- **dairy-free chocolate chips**
- **crushed graham crackers or gluten-free cookies**
- **chopped dates**
- **nut or seed butter**

SERVES 4

PER SERVING: calories 125, fat 1 g, protein 1 g, carbohydrates 32 g, dietary fiber 3 g

PREP TIME: 5 minutes

In a food processor, puree the bananas for 1 to 2 minutes, until smooth and creamy. Add any add-ins, if using. Process again and serve immediately.

salted caramel hot cocoa

Hot cocoa can be tricky to make delicious for those on a dairy-free diet. This version is not only creamy and chocolaty, but has a sweet-salty kick that makes it extra special. To get this just right, you'll need a candy thermometer.

ingredients

1   cup raw cane sugar

1   teaspoon pure vanilla extract

1½ teaspoons fleur de sel or other flaky sea salt

2   tablespoons nonhydrogenated margarine

4   cups soymilk

3   ounces nondairy bittersweet baking chocolate bar, chopped

   Nondairy whipped topping, for garnish

   Finely chopped bittersweet chocolate, for garnish

SERVES 8

PER SERVING: calories 247, fat 10 g, protein 5 g, carbohydrates 38 g, dietary fiber 2 g

PREP + COOK TIME: 30 minutes

1. In a medium deep pot, add the sugar, vanilla, salt, margarine, and 1 cup of the soymilk. Heat over medium-low heat, stirring constantly, and cook until the caramel reaches 217°F on a candy thermometer. If the temperature raises above 218°F this can cause the caramel to taste somewhat burnt. Remove from the heat.

2. Fill the bottom of a double boiler with a few inches of water over medium-low heat. Have the chopped chocolate waiting in the top section of the double boiler, but do not place it over the hot water yet. In a separate medium saucepan, bring the remaining 3 cups of soymilk to a boil, then pour it over the chopped chocolate. Gently mix and set over the boiling water in the double boiler, stirring until the chocolate is completely melted.

3. Slowly pour the chocolate milk into the caramel, mixing as you go to combine completely. Top with the whipped topping and bittersweet chocolate.

WHOLE-WHEAT LEMON SHORTBREAD,
PAGE 130

raw summer peach tart

Savor summertime's bounty of fresh fruit with this unbaked dessert. A honey-nut crust adds a little texture to the creamy, agave-sweetened cashew filling, making it the perfect bed for tender white peaches. Please note that if you want to prepare your own cashews, they must first be soaked for eight hours.

ingredients

CASHEW CREAM FILLING

2½	cups cashews, or 2 cups cashew butter
8	Medjool dates, pitted
6	tablespoons agave nectar
1	tablespoon fresh lemon juice
¼	teaspoon salt
¼	cup coconut oil, at room temperature
1	vanilla bean
3	tablespoons unsweetened almond milk (optional)

PREP TIME: 30 minutes + 1 hour to chill

1. To make the cashew cream filling, if using cashews, soak for 8 hours in 6 cups water, then rinse a few times until the water is no longer cloudy. Drain fully.

2. Soak the dates in a small bowl of water for 15 minutes. Drain the dates and discard the water.

3. Combine the cashews or cashew butter, dates, agave nectar, lemon juice, salt, and coconut oil in a blender. Cut the vanilla bean in half lengthwise. Use a spoon to scoop out the inside of the bean and drop the tiny vanilla seeds into the blender as well. Save the vanilla pod to use another time.

4. Pulse until you've got a smooth consistency, scraping down the sides of the blender jar with a spatula as needed. Add a few tablespoons of the almond milk if you prefer a thinner cream. The cream will keep in an airtight container in the refrigerator for up to 1 week.

5. To make the honey nut crust, chop the pecans into a coarse meal using a food processor. Pour the pecan meal into a medium bowl and set aside.

HONEY NUT CRUST

2   **cups pecans (halves or pieces will work)**

4   **Medjool dates, pitted and chopped**

2   **teaspoons coconut oil, at room temperature**

2   **tablespoons raw honey**

2   **teaspoons ground cinnamon**

1   **tablespoon cocoa powder**

¼   **teaspoon sea salt**

½   **vanilla bean**

3   **fresh peaches, peeled and cut into thick slices**

SERVES 8

PER SERVING: calories 555, fat 43 g, protein 9 g, carbohydrates 44 g, dietary fiber 6 g

6. Add the dates, coconut oil, honey, cinnamon, cocoa powder, and salt to the jar of the blender. Cut the vanilla bean in half lengthwise. Use a spoon to scoop out the inside of the bean and drop the seeds into the blender. Save the vanilla pod to use another time. Pulse a few times until you've got a relatively smooth paste.

7. Scrape the date mixture into the pecan meal, and mix well to combine. Press into a 10-inch pie plate. Cover and refrigerate until ready to use.

8. To assemble the tart, pour the cashew cream filling into the prepared crust and smooth with a spatula. Arrange the peach slices on the top of the filling in attractive circles.

9. Refrigerate the tart for 1 hour before serving. It will keep in the refrigerator for 1 week if tightly covered.

almost-raw chocolate cashew fudge

Made with all-natural ingredients and sweeteners, this healthier take on a classic sweet treat won't leave you feeling like you've overindulged—unless you gobble up the whole pan, of course! You can use any nut or seed butter you like in this recipe. Cashews will yield the creamiest results, while other nuts will add more texture. Note that if you want to prepare your own cashews, they must first be soaked for eight hours.

ingredients

2   cups cashews, or 1½ cups cashew butter

6   tablespoons agave nectar

¼   cup coconut oil, at room temperature

½   teaspoon salt

⅛   teaspoon vanilla extract

½   cup unsweetened cocoa powder

MAKES 12 PIECES OF FUDGE
PER SERVING: calories 210, fat 16 g, protein 4 g, carbohydrates 18 g, dietary fiber 2 g

PREP TIME: 10 minutes + 30 minutes chilling time

1. If using cashews, soak for 8 hours in 6 cups of water, then rinse a few times until the water is no longer cloudy. Drain fully.

2. In a blender, combine the cashews or cashew butter, agave, coconut oil, salt, and vanilla. Blend to a smooth paste. (If you are using cashew butter instead of soaked cashews, you can mix in a bowl instead of a blender.) Add the cocoa powder and continue to blend until you've got a smooth, velvety texture.

3. Scoop the fudge into a bowl and place in the refrigerator for 20 minutes to solidify and reduce the stickiness. Line a plate with a piece of parchment.

4. Once the fudge has hardened a bit, scoop out 12 teaspoon-size portions onto the parchment. Place the fudge back in the refrigerator for 10 minutes. When cool, roll the scoops into the shape of a ball with your hands. Store in the refrigerator in an airtight container for up to 3 weeks.

almond flour honey cakes

With just a touch of honey, these little individually baked cakes are perfect for after dinner. Tender and warm, they'll send your kids off to bed with visions of cinnamon and nutmeg dancing in their heads.

ingredients

Butter or nonhydroge-nated, soy-free marga-rine, for coating and serving

2 cups almond flour plus ½ cup for preparing ramekins

¼ cup sliced almonds

½ teaspoon ground cinnamon

¼ teaspoon ground nutmeg

¾ teaspoon baking soda

½ teaspoon salt

½ cup honey

2 large eggs, beaten

¾ cup low-fat yogurt or coconut yogurt

½ teaspoon vanilla extract

Honey, for drizzling

SERVES 8
PER SERVING: calories 235,
 fat 14 g, protein 8 g,
carbohydrates 24 g,
dietary fiber 2 g

PREP TIME: 10 minutes
COOK TIME: 40 minutes

1. Preheat the oven to 325°F. Coat 8 (6-ounce) ramekins with the butter or margarine, and dust with the almond flour. Sprinkle the bottom of each with the sliced almonds.

2. In a bowl, combine the almond flour, cinnamon, nutmeg, baking soda, and salt. Stir until completely combined. Add the honey, eggs, yogurt, and vanilla and mix well.

3. Spoon the batter into the prepared ramekins until they are two-thirds full. Place the ramekins on a rimmed baking sheet large enough to hold them. Bake for 40 minutes, until the tops are golden-brown. Allow to cool for 15 minutes.

4. Run a butter knife around the edges of each cake to loosen it, then invert the ramekin on a plate and tap the bottom to release the cake from the dish. Serve hot with butter or margarine and honey on the side. In the summer, top with white peaches or nectarines.

gluten-free pie crust

The key to making a flaky pie crust—gluten-free or otherwise—is supercold ingredients. For best results, chill everything in the freezer for 15 minutes before combining. Use this single crust as a base for Spiced Pumpkin Pie (page 140) or your family's favorite pie. You can double the quantities for a double crust. Please note that this recipe calls for potato starch, not potato flour.

ingredients

- ¾ **cup sorghum flour**
- ¼ **cup potato starch**
- ¼ **cup tapioca starch**
- ¾ **teaspoon xanthan gum**
- ¼ **teaspoon salt**
- ¼ **cup soy-free, nonhydrogenated margarine, chilled and cut into small pieces**
- ¼ **cup nonhydrogenated shortening, chilled and cut into small pieces**
- 3 **tablespoons ice water**

MAKES 1 PIE CRUST
SERVES 8
PER SERVING: calories 185, fat 12 g, protein 1 g, carbohydrates 17 g, dietary fiber 1 g

PREP TIME: 35 minutes, mostly unattended

1. In a food processor, add the sorghum flour, potato starch, tapioca starch, xanthan gum, and salt. Pulse to combine.

2. Add the margarine and shortening and pulse again, until small crumbs begin to form.

3. Add the water and pulse a few more times, until the dough begins to clump together.

4. Remove the dough from the food processor and flatten into a disk. Wrap in parchment paper and refrigerate for at least 30 minutes before rolling out on a sorghum-floured surface and placing on a pie plate. The crust is ready to fill or prebake, depending on the recipe you're using. To prebake, use a fork to poke the bottom of the crust several times. Place in a 350°F oven for 15 to 20 minutes, until the crust is lightly golden.

spiced pumpkin pie

The holidays are even happier when everyone can enjoy this favorite—though we wouldn't be surprised if you end up making this traditional pie all autumn long! Serve with whipped cream, if desired, or dairy-free whipped soy or rice cream.

ingredients

1	unbaked Gluten-Free Pie Crust (page 139) or your favorite 9-inch pie shell
1	(12-ounce) package soft silken tofu, drained
1	(15-ounce) can pure pumpkin puree (about 2 cups)
¾	cup pure maple syrup
¼	cup packed dark brown sugar
¼	cup cornstarch
1	teaspoon vanilla extract
½	teaspoon salt
1½	teaspoons ground cinnamon
½	teaspoon ground ginger
¼	teaspoon ground nutmeg
⅛	teaspoon ground allspice
⅛	teaspoon ground cloves

PREP TIME: 5 minutes
BAKE TIME: 45 minutes

1. Preheat the oven to 350°F. Set out the prepared pie crust.

2. In a food processor or blender, add the tofu and process until completely smooth. Add the pumpkin, maple syrup, brown sugar, cornstarch, vanilla, salt, cinnamon, ginger, nutmeg, allspice, and cloves and process again until combined.

3. Pour the pumpkin filling into the pie shell, and bake for 45 to 50 minutes, until the center remains mostly stable when you move the pie plate back and forth. Chill for 1 to 2 hours before serving.

SERVES 8
PER SERVING: calories 272, fat 14 g, protein 5 g, carbohydrates 49 g, dietary fiber 4 g

all about sugar

Sugar may strike fear into the hearts of nutrition-minded parents, but it doesn't have to. Once you know what you're dealing with, you can decide what to use—and how much.

The common white (or raw brown) crystals we stir into our coffee and bake into our kids' cookies is a natural substance derived from either the sugarcane or sugar beet. The plants are sliced and soaked (beets) or shredded and squeezed (cane), then spun in a contraption to shake off the molasses. A hot-water spray separates out the white crystals that, when dried, we know as table sugar, or *sucrose*.

All sugars (and there are several different kinds) are part of a group of edible molecules known as simple carbohydrates. They're termed "simple" because they're made up of only one or two molecules bound together. Complex carbohydrates (like whole grains), by contrast, can be composed of thousands of sugar molecules.

Many of the health concerns about table sugar stem from its being so simple in its molecular construction that it breaks down extremely quickly and is rapidly swept into the bloodstream, explains Paul Kaplowitz, MD, chief of endocrinology at Children's National Medical Center in Washington, DC. Too much simple sugar of any kind in the bloodstream at one time can raise the body's blood sugar above healthy levels. When this happens, it sets off a complicated process by which the pancreas must produce and release the hormone insulin, explains Kaplowitz. "Insulin sweeps excess glucose out of your blood and into storage in your liver, muscles, and fatty tissues," he says. And those extra calories from the sugar—if they're not burned off—get stored as fat in the body.

The good news: "You don't need to be iron-fisted and say 'No more sugar in our house!'" says New York City–based registered dietitian Cynthia Sass. The key is moderation, and keeping your family's intake to natural (not added) sugar as much as you can. Go organic, too: If it has that USDA Organic seal, you can feel confident that the original plant was grown responsibly and healthfully. For a list of natural alternatives to white sugar, see page 220.

snacks

SOMETIMES IT feels like kids eat snacks more than they eat meals—at school, after school, at soccer practice . . . And in fact, kids consume about 600 calories from snacks every day, a recent study found. Since you're not likely to bring down the snack culture single-handedly, it's so important to make sure those aren't empty calories.

Think about snacks as mini meals: The best ones are small, fun portions of food you wouldn't mind seeing in your child's lunch box or on the dinner table, like our Rice Ball Surprise and Spiced Carrot Fries. But not always, because fun foods are fine to rotate in, as well. The important thing is to teach your child which is which. A few of these recipes wouldn't pass the "would you serve it for dinner" test, as much as your kids might like chocolate and cinnamon every night. Consider those special-occasion snacks, and remember: They're still way better than the processed, artificially flavored stuff targeted at kids.

Another reason to love DIY snacks is that they tend to be a lot less time-intensive than a full meal. That'll make your life a lot easier when you find yourself agreeing to bring a snack to soccer practice more often than the other moms do, just so that your food-sensitive kid can be sure to have something yummy!

G=GLUTEN-FREE

D=DAIRY-FREE

N=NUT-FREE

E=EGG-FREE

S=SOY-FREE

KEY

Chewy Strawberry Fruit Leather G, D, N, E, S 145

Pear Dunkers with Cashew-Cinnamon Yogurt Sauce G, D, E, S 146

Fruit and Nut Snackballs G, D, E, S 148

Chickpea Herb Crackers G, D, N, E, S 151

Granola Squares G, D, N, E, S 152

Pumpkin Mini Muffins G, D, N, E, S 153

Good-for-You Nachos G, D, N, E, S 155

Savory Roasted Chickpeas G, D, N, E 156

Walnut-Stuffed Figs G, D, E, S 157

Spiced Carrot Fries G, D, N, E, S 158

Rice Ball Surprise G, D, N, E option, S option 160

Zucchini Boats G, D, N, E, S 162

Buffalo Green Beans G, D option, N, E, S 163

Chocolate Cinnamon Crisps G, D option, N, E, S 165

Apple Sun Smiles G, D, N, E, S 166

Indoors S'mores G, D option, N option, E, S 167

Fruity Guac G, N, E, S 168

Saucy Pears and Butternut Squash G, D, N, E, S 170

Crunchy Maple–Walnut Popcorn G, D, E, S 172

chewy strawberry fruit leather

Making your own fruit leather is easier than it sounds. Try making a few variations the first time so you can determine how much honey and lemon juice is a hit with your family. Other fruits or fruit combinations work well, too.

ingredients

Canola oil, for coating the parchment paper

1 **pint strawberries, hulled and halved**

½ **to 2 tablespoons honey**

½ **to 2 tablespoons fresh lemon juice**

PREP TIME: 10 minutes
DEHYDRATING TIME: 6 to 14 hours, depending on your oven

1. Preheat your oven to its lowest setting, from 110°F to 170°F. Line a rimmed baking sheet with parchment paper, and lightly coat the paper with canola oil.

2. In a food processor, puree the strawberries until completely smooth. Add the honey and lemon juice to taste. Process until combined.

3. Pour the strawberry puree onto the baking sheet, and use a spatula to evenly spread the puree less than ⅛ inch thick.

4. Dehydrate in the oven for 6 to 14 hours, or until the fruit has formed into a semisticky leather. If your oven temperature is at or near 170°F, leave the oven door cracked open to allow extra heat to escape, preventing the fruit from cooking instead of dehydrating.

5. Slice into 8 long rectangles and wrap each piece in parchment paper. Stored in an airtight container, fruit leather will last up to 1 month.

MAKES 8 PIECES
PER PIECE: calories 21, fat 0 g, protein 0 g, carbohydrates 6 g, dietary fiber 1 g

pear dunkers with cashew-cinnamon yogurt sauce

This nutritious snack comes together super quickly, and kids tend to love sweetened-up nut butters. If your cashew butter has been in the fridge, warm it in the microwave for 10 or 15 seconds to soften it.

ingredients

1   (6-ounce) container plain dairy yogurt or coconut milk yogurt

2   tablespoons cashew butter, at room temperature

1   tablespoon honey

¼   teaspoon ground cinnamon

2   pears, sliced into 1-inch wedges

SERVES 4

PER SERVING: calories 139, fat 5 g, protein 4 g, carbohydrates 22 g, dietary fiber 2 g

PREP TIME: 5 minutes

Add the yogurt, cashew butter, honey, and cinnamon to a medium bowl. Whisk to combine. Adjust the honey to taste. Serve with pear slices for dipping.

fruit and nut snackballs

Your kids won't want to wait for your next hike to try these trail mix–inspired treats. They pack long-lasting energy in a small, fun-to-eat package. They're especially fun for kids to make, from crushing the almonds to rolling the ingredients into the cute little balls.

ingredients

PREP TIME: 10 minutes

1   **cup whole raw almonds**

1   **cup pitted dates, finely chopped**

½   **cup dried cherries, finely chopped**

½   **teaspoon vanilla extract**

¼   **teaspoon almond extract**

¼   **teaspoon salt**

Canola oil, for your hands

1. In a food processor, chop the almonds coarsely. Transfer to a medium bowl.

2. Add the dates, cherries, vanilla, almond extract, and salt to the chopped almonds. Mix well to combine.

3. Lightly coat your hands to keep the mixture from sticking to them, then roll the mixture into 14 golf ball–size balls. Serve.

MAKES 14 SNACKBALLS
PER SNACKBALL:
calories 110, fat 5 g,
protein 3 g,
carbohydrates 15 g,
dietary fiber 2 g

COOKING WITH KIDS

teach your child to crush nuts

There are plenty of ways to break nuts down into smaller pieces: You can chop them, pulverize them in a food processor, or go the more kid-friendly route of smashing them in a plastic bag.

STEP 1 Have your child measure the nuts with a measuring cup and pour them into a large, zip-top bag. Before zipping the bag shut, have her squeeze out all the air in the bag.

STEP 2 Your child can place the bag flat on a surface. Then with a rolling pin or mallet, she can roll or hammer the nuts into tiny pieces. Now the nuts are ready to make snackballs, add to cookie batter, or toss in salads!

chickpea
herb crackers

Chickpea flour lends extra flavor and protein to these gluten-free crisps. These are tasty alone or with your favorite dip or cheese. Please note that this recipe calls for potato starch, not potato flour.

ingredients

PREP TIME: 20 minutes
BAKE TIME: 15 minutes

¼ **cup olive oil, plus more for coating the pan**

1 **cup chickpea flour, plus more for dusting**

½ **cup cornmeal**

¼ **cup potato starch**

¼ **cup tapioca starch**

1 **tablespoon dried rosemary**

1 **teaspoon salt**

1 **teaspoon baking powder**

½ **teaspoon xanthan gum**

Grated zest of 1 small lemon

½ **cup plus 1 tablespoon water**

1. Preheat the oven to 425°F. Lightly coat two rimmed baking sheets with olive oil.

2. In a medium bowl, add the chickpea flour, cornmeal, potato starch, tapioca starch, rosemary, salt, baking powder, xanthan gum, and lemon zest. Whisk to combine, then add the water and olive oil. Mix the dough well.

3. Dust a flat surface with chickpea flour. Tear off a small ball of dough (about the size of a lemon), and use a rolling pin to roll as thin as possible, ¹⁄₁₆ to ⅛ inch thick. The gluten-free dough is delicate; working with smaller pieces, instead of rolling out all the dough at once, will prevent it from tearing. Place the rolled-out dough on the baking sheet. Use a knife to score lines where you'll later break the cracker apart to make smaller crackers. Repeat with the remaining dough.

4. Bake for 14 to 16 minutes, until the crackers just begin to brown. Allow to cool completely, then break into small crackers along the score marks. Store in an airtight container for up to 2 days.

SERVES 12

PER SERVING: calories 110, fat 5 g, protein 2 g, carbohydrates 14 g, dietary fiber 1 g

granola squares

Delicious, portable, and packed with nutrition, these squares are adaptable to your family's taste. Swap out the apricots and sunflower seeds for any dried fruit and seed/nut combination you like.

ingredients

⅓ **cup canola oil, plus more for coating the pan**

1½ **cups gluten-free rolled oats**

1½ **cups gluten-free oat flour**

1 **cup dried apricots, chopped**

½ **cup sunflower seeds**

½ **teaspoon salt**

½ **cup honey**

1 **tablespoon ground flaxseed whisked with 2 tablespoons water**

½ **teaspoon vanilla extract**

¼ **teaspoon almond extract**

MAKES 16 SQUARES

PER SQUARE: calories 178, fat 8 g, protein 4 g, carbohydrates 26 g, dietary fiber 3 g

PREP TIME: 5 minutes
BAKE TIME: 35 minutes

1. Preheat the oven to 350°F. Line an 8-inch square pan with foil so that the edges of the foil hang over the sides of the pan, and lightly coat the foil with canola oil.

2. In a medium bowl, combine the rolled oats, oat flour, dried apricots, sunflower seeds, and salt.

3. In a small bowl, whisk the honey, canola oil, flaxseed mixture, vanilla, and almond extract. Pour the wet ingredients over the dry and mix until well-combined.

4. Press the dough into the prepared pan and bake for 30 to 35 minutes, until the edges are just golden-brown.

5. Allow to cool completely, then remove from the pan by lifting the foil edges out. Cut into squares and serve, or store in an airtight container for up to 3 days.

pumpkin
mini muffins

Smeared with your child's favorite nut or seed butter, these wholesome muffins make a perfect autumn after-school bite. This recipe also works to make about 10 regular-size muffins, which need an additional 8 to 10 minutes of baking time. Please note that this recipe calls for potato starch, not potato flour.

ingredients

- ⅓ **cup canola oil, plus more for coating the muffin cups**
- 1 **cup sorghum flour**
- ¼ **cup tapioca starch**
- ¼ **cup potato starch**
- 1 **teaspoon baking powder**
- ½ **teaspoon salt**
- ½ **teaspoon xanthan gum**
- ½ **teaspoon ground ginger**
- ¼ **teaspoon ground nutmeg**
- ½ **cup raw cane sugar**
- ½ **cup pure pumpkin puree**
- 1 **tablespoon ground flaxseeds whisked with 2 tablespoons warm water**
- 1 **teaspoon vanilla extract**

MAKES 22 MINI MUFFINS

PER MINI MUFFIN:
calories 83, fat 4 g,
protein 1 g,
carbohydrates 13 g,
dietary fiber 1 g

PREP TIME: 5 minutes
BAKE TIME: 17 to 20 minutes

1. Preheat the oven to 350°F. Lightly coat 22 mini muffin cups with canola oil.

2. In a medium bowl, combine the sorghum flour, tapioca starch, potato starch, baking powder, salt, xanthan gum, ginger, and nutmeg.

3. In a large bowl, whisk the canola oil and sugar. Add the pumpkin puree, flaxseed mixture, and vanilla and mix to combine.

4. Add the dry ingredients to the wet and mix until just combined. Scoop rounded tablespoons of batter into the muffin cups (they should be nearly full). Bake for 17 to 20 minutes (25 to 30 minutes for full-size muffins), until a toothpick inserted into the center comes out clean. Allow to cool completely before serving.

teach your child to scoop an avocado

STEP 1 After slicing the avocado in half, give each half to your child. While the avocado flesh is still in the skin, she can use a butter knife to slice the flesh four or five times lengthwise and crosswise, working around the pit.

STEP 2 With a large spoon, your child can scoop the sliced avocado out of its skin and into a bowl. She can user her fingers or a spoon to remove the pit from the flesh—but be careful, it's slippery!

STEP 3 Have your child squeeze the lime juice over the avocado, which will help the avocado stay bright green. Now it's ready to eat!

good-for-you nachos

All nachos are tasty, but most aren't very healthy or allergy-friendly, since they're usually loaded with cheese. This version is piled high with veggies and gets richness and flavor from refried beans and avocado.

ingredients

Canola oil, for coating the baking sheet

4 **ounces gluten-free corn tortilla chips**

1 **(16-ounce) can vegetarian refried beans**

½ **avocado, diced**

1 **teaspoon fresh lime juice**

Salt

1 **cup shredded romaine lettuce**

½ **Roma tomato, diced**

SERVES 6

PER SERVING: calories 171, fat 8 g, protein 5 g, carbohydrates 22 g, dietary fiber 5 g

PREP TIME: 5 minutes
BAKE TIME: 10 minutes

1. Preheat the oven to 400°F. Lightly coat a rimmed baking sheet with canola oil.

2. Spread the chips on the baking sheet in an even layer. Top with the refried beans and bake for 8 to 10 minutes, until the beans are warmed through.

3. While the nachos bake, make the guacamole. Combine the avocado, lime juice, and salt to taste in a bowl and lightly mash with a fork.

4. Top the nachos with the guacamole, lettuce, and plum tomato. Serve hot.

savory roasted chickpeas

Salty, slightly smoky roast chickpeas are just as addictive as potato chips—or popcorn, which your kids won't miss once they start popping these into their mouths. Leftovers taste delicious added to a hummus- and veggie-filled pita sandwich.

ingredients

- 1 (15-ounce) can chickpeas, rinsed and drained
- 1 tablespoon plus 1 teaspoon wheat-free tamari
- 2 teaspoons olive oil
- ½ teaspoon smoked sweet paprika

PREP TIME: 5 minutes
BAKE TIME: 20 minutes

1. Preheat the oven or toaster oven to 425°F. Set out a rimmed baking sheet.

2. Dry the chickpeas with a kitchen towel or lettuce spinner. Place the chickpeas on the baking sheet. Add the tamari, olive oil, and paprika and toss gently to combine.

3. Bake for 20 minutes, tossing with a spatula halfway through, until lightly browned. Serve. Refrigerate leftovers in an airtight container for up to 4 days.

SERVES 4

PER SERVING: calories 130, fat 3 g, protein 5 g, carbohydrates 21 g, dietary fiber 4 g

walnut-stuffed figs

These sweet, easy-to-prepare bites might taste like candy, but they're actually packed with great nutrition. The walnuts are loaded with protein and omega-3s, while the figs offer a healthy dose of fiber and iron.

ingredients

- **12 dried Calimyrna figs**
- ½ **cup walnuts, chopped**
- **2 to 4 tablespoons honey**
- ½ **teaspoon ground cinnamon**
- ¼ **teaspoon salt**

PREP TIME: 10 minutes

1. Slice each fig nearly in half at the base, leaving the top of each fig whole.

2. In a small bowl, combine the walnuts, honey to taste, cinnamon, and salt. Stir to combine.

3. With your fingers or a small spoon, stuff each fig with an equal amount of the walnut mixture. Serve.

MAKES 12 STUFFED FIGS
PER FIG: calories 91, fat 4 g, protein 2 g, carbohydrates 16 g, dietary fiber 2 g

spiced
carrot fries

The warming cumin and cinnamon in these roasted veggie sticks are perfect on a cold day. They add a kid-friendly zest to carrot sticks, which can start to get a little old on their own. Serve alone, or with Tahini-Lime Sauce (page 43) for dipping.

ingredients

2   **large carrots, peeled and sliced into matchsticks**

1   **tablespoon olive oil**

½   **teaspoon ground cumin**

¼   **teaspoon ground cinnamon**

   Salt and freshly ground black pepper

PREP TIME: 5 minutes
BAKE TIME: 22 minutes

1. Preheat the oven to 425°F. Set out a rimmed baking sheet.

2. In a medium bowl, add the carrots, olive oil, cumin, cinnamon, and salt and pepper to taste. Toss to coat the carrots.

3. Transfer the carrots to the baking sheet, making sure no carrots overlap. Bake for 20 to 22 minutes, tossing with tongs halfway through, until lightly browned. Serve.

SERVES 4
PER SERVING: calories 45, fat 4 g, protein .5 g, carbohydrates 3 g, dietary fiber 1 g

rice ball surprise

Called onigiri *in Japan, these little rice balls can be filled with anything—smoked salmon, jam, sweet corn, you name it. Finding the little treat inside is fun for kids, and if your child isn't already a sushi eater, these tasty treats are a great way to introduce your child to some of the flavors of Japan. You can use short-grain brown rice for making* onigiri, *as long as you don't wash the rice before cooking. Brown rice* onigiri *may not be as starchy as those made with short-grain white rice, but they should hold their shape.*

ingredients

2	**cups uncooked sushi rice**
4	**sheets nori seaweed wrappers**
1	**can water-packed tuna, drained**
¼	**cup light mayonnaise or vegan mayonnaise**
2	**teaspoons mustard**
¼	**teaspoon salt**
¼	**cup black or white sesame seeds**

PREP TIME: 20 minutes
COOK TIME: 45 minutes (for rice)

1. Prepare the sushi rice according to the package directions, but do not rinse the rice before cooking so that it retains some of its stickiness. Spread on a rimmed baking sheet and allow to cool for 5 minutes.

2. Meanwhile, cut 2 sheets of nori in half diagonally, to make 4 triangles. Cut the remaining sheets into 8 2-inch-wide strips.

3. In a small bowl, combine the tuna, mayonnaise, mustard, and salt. Mix well and set aside.

4. Fill a bowl with warm water. Dip your hands in it and scoop up about ½ cup of rice. Spread the rice into a thick patty on your palm, and with your other hand place 2 tablespoons of tuna in the middle. Form the rice into a ball around the filling, and pack it together well. Then, follow the instructions to construct your *onigiri* into a disk, triangle, or cylinder shape. You'll have enough nori to create 4 of each shape.

MAKES 12 RICE BALLS
PER RICE BALL: calories 183, fat 5 g, protein 7 g, carbohydrates 27 g, dietary fiber 1 g

OTHER ONIGIRI FILLINGS

Smoked salmon

Peanut butter or sunflower butter and jelly

Whole berries

Thick pudding or custard

Crushed fruit, such as peaches or pineapple

Shredded barbecued chicken

Sautéed onions and mushrooms

Sweet corn

Grilled shrimp

Cooked ground beef with a touch of barbecue sauce

TO MAKE A DISK-SHAPED ONIGIRI

Flatten the ball of rice to create a puck-shaped disk and sprinkle lightly with sesame seeds. Wrap a 2-inch strip of nori around the rice, across the diameter of the disk, and secure using a wet finger to seal the nori to itself.

TO MAKE A TRIANGLE-SHAPED ONIGIRI

Flatten the ball of rice somewhat to create a puck-shaped disk. Using your palms, form the rice into a triangle shape, packing well to form a solid mass. Sprinkle lightly with sesame seeds. Take 1 triangle of nori and lay it flat on the counter, placing the onigiri in the middle of the sheet, standing up like a Christmas tree. Fold the triangle around the onigiri so that the top corner of the triangle is poking out of the nori wrapper. Secure, using a wet finger to seal the nori to itself.

TO MAKE A CYLINDER-SHAPED ONIGIRI

Form the rice ball into a thick log-shape and sprinkle lightly with sesame seeds. Wrap a 2-inch strip of nori around the log and secure using a wet finger to seal the nori to itself.

zucchini boats

Zucchini makes a fun—and good-for-you—hummus delivery system. If you're super pressed for time, use a tub of all-natural, store-bought hummus.

ingredients

1	**(15-ounce) can chickpeas, rinsed and drained**
2	**tablespoons tahini**
2	**tablespoons fresh lemon juice**
2	**tablespoons water**
1	**tablespoon olive oil**
1	**clove garlic**
½	**teaspoon salt**
2	**large zucchini, halved crosswise and again lengthwise**
	Smoked paprika, for garnish

PREP TIME: 10 minutes

1. To make the hummus, add the chickpeas, tahini, lemon juice, water, olive oil, garlic, and salt to a food processor. Process until smooth. Set aside.

2. With a small spoon, scoop out ¼ to ½ inch of the flesh of each zucchini piece to form hollowed-out boats.

3. Spoon the hummus evenly into the zucchini boats. Sprinkle with paprika and serve.

MAKES 8 ZUCCHINI BOATS
PER ZUCCHINI BOAT:
calories 104, fat 4 g,
protein 4 g,
carbohydrates 14 g,
dietary fiber 3 g

buffalo green beans

The classic Buffalo flavor tastes just as good on crisp green beans as it does on crunchy chicken. And while chicken wings might be better suited for a meal, lighter green beans make for a flavorful—and satisfying—snack. If you happen to have any left over, pack them in your child's lunch the next day.

ingredients

- 1 **pound green beans, trimmed**
- 3 **tablespoons unsalted butter or soy-free, nonhydrogenated margarine**
- ¼ **cup hot sauce**

PREP TIME: 10 minutes
COOK TIME: 5 minutes

1. Bring a large pot of salted water to a boil. Add the beans and cook for about 2 minutes, until bright green and tender. Drain.

2. While the beans are cooking, melt the butter in a medium skillet over medium-high heat. Add the hot sauce and stir to combine. Add the drained beans and cook, stirring constantly, for about 2 minutes, until the sauce is slightly reduced and coats the beans. Serve immediately.

SERVES 6

PER SERVING: calories 75, fat 6 g, protein 2 g, carbohydrates 6 g, dietary fiber 3 g

chocolate cinnamon crisps

The crunchiness in these snacks makes the sweetness extra satisfying. Many corn tortillas are gluten-free. Just be sure to check the packaging, as some are made in facilities with wheat as well.

ingredients

2 **tablespoons raw cane sugar**

¼ **teaspoon ground cinnamon**

¼ **teaspoon cocoa powder**

1 **tablespoon olive oil or butter, melted**

4 **gluten-free corn tortillas**

Powdered sugar (optional)

Ice cream topping, warmed (optional)

Fresh strawberries, sprinkled with sugar and lightly mashed (optional)

SERVES 4

PER SERVING: calories 103, fat 4 g, protein 1 g, carbohydrates 17 g, dietary fiber 2 g

PREP TIME: 5 minutes
COOK TIME: 10 minutes

1. Preheat the oven to 425°F. Stir together the sugar, cinnamon, and cocoa powder in a small bowl.

2. Brush one side of each tortilla with olive oil or butter. Sprinkle the tortillas with the sugar mixture. Use a pizza cutter or knife to cut each tortilla into 6 wedges. Place the wedges in a single layer on a rimmed baking sheet. Bake for about 10 minutes, or until the wedges are crisp.

3. Remove from the oven and let cool. If desired, sift the powdered sugar and/or drizzle warm ice cream topping over the wedges. You can also serve with a small bowl of mashed strawberries for dipping.

apple
sun smiles

Once your child helps you construct these apple-slice snackwiches, don't be surprised if he discovers how much each slice resembles a smile! Hold them up to your lips, grin, and chow down.

ingredients

3   **tablespoons sunflower butter**

3   **tablespoons crushed allergy-friendly granola**

   Dash of cinnamon

1   **apple, cut into 16 slices**

SERVES 8

PER SERVING: calories 58, fat 4 g, protein 2 g, carbohydrates 5 g, dietary fiber 1 g

PREP TIME: 10 minutes

1.   Stir together the sunflower butter, granola, and cinnamon in a small bowl.

2.   Spread the mixture on one side of 8 of the apple slices. Top each with the remaining slices.

indoors s'mores

Have kids help you crush the graham crackers and you'll be halfway to the way-better-than-a-microwave way of eating s'mores. The pretzels, if you use them, add a great salty kick to this sweet treat.

ingredients

- 1¾ cups crushed gluten-free graham crackers
- 6 tablespoons butter or soy-free, nonhydrogenated margarine, melted
- 1 cup gluten-free, dairy-free, soy-free chocolate chips
- ¼ cup sunflower seed butter, almond butter, or peanut butter
- ½ cup coarsely crushed gluten-free pretzels (optional)
- 1 cup miniature marshmallows

MAKES 16 SQUARES
PER SQUARE: calories 171, fat 11 g, protein 3 g, carbohydrates 17 g, dietary fiber 2 g

PREP TIME: 5 minutes
COOK TIME: 20 minutes

1. Preheat the oven to 350°F. Place the graham cracker crumbs in an 8-inch square baking dish. Pour the melted butter over the crumbs and stir well to combine. Pat the mixture evenly in the pan. Bake for 8 minutes, or until lightly browned. Remove from the oven, and increase the oven temperature to 400°F.

2. Meanwhile, combine the chocolate chips and sunflower seed butter in a small saucepan. Cook and stir over low heat for 2 to 3 minutes, until melted and smooth. Carefully pour the chocolate mixture over the graham cracker crust.

3. If desired, sprinkle crushed pretzels over the chocolate. Top with marshmallows. Return the pan to the oven. Bake for 5 to 8 minutes, until the marshmallows are lightly browned. Cool completely on a wire rack. Cut into 2-inch squares. Leftovers will keep for up to 5 days in an airtight container.

fruity guac

This is a sweet twist on guacamole that appeals to a kid's sweet tooth without making you worry about sugar and unhealthy fat. If your avocados need ripening, place them in a paper bag with a banana and seal shut. Check back 12 to 24 hours later for a ripened avocado. The pomegranate seeds add a touch of tartness, but if they aren't in season, just omit from the recipe.

ingredients

- 2 **avocados, pitted, peeled, and diced**
- 2 **bananas, diced**
- **Juice of 2 limes (about ¼ cup)**
- ½ **teaspoon salt**
- 2 **tablespoons ricotta cheese**
- ⅓ **cup pomegranate seeds (optional)**

SERVES 6

PER SERVING: calories 152, fat 10 g, protein 2 g, carbohydrates 16 g, dietary fiber 6 g

PREP TIME: 10 minutes

1. In a small bowl, use a fork to mash the avocados, bananas, lime juice, and salt into a chunky consistency.

2. Add the ricotta and stir to combine. Taste and season with additional salt or lime juice, if needed.

3. Top with the pomegranate seeds, if using, and serve with your favorite whole-grain chips.

saucy pears and butternut squash

Applesauce getting a little old? Mix things up with this kid-pleasing puree. The cooking time is long, but it's mostly unattended—put this together while you're making dinner and you'll have snacks ready for tomorrow.

ingredients

1   (3-pound) butternut squash

2   Bartlett pears

3   tablespoons olive oil

1   teaspoon ground cinnamon

1   teaspoon sea salt

PREP TIME: 15 minutes
COOK TIME: 2 hours

1. Preheat the oven to 400°F. Place one oven rack in the middle of the oven, and another near the top of the oven. Or, if your oven has the heating element at the top, place the second rack near the bottom, away from the heating element.

2. Cut the squash in half lengthwise and scoop out the seeds with a spoon. Line a large rimmed baking sheet with parchment paper, and place the squash cut side up in the pan.

3. Peel the pears and cut into quarters, removing the cores and seeds. Line a small baking dish with parchment and place the pears inside.

4. Place the squash on the middle oven rack, and the pears on the rack farther away from the heating element. Roast the pears for 45 minutes, remove from the oven, and set aside. The squash will start to bubble up and turn a dark orange-brown. After 2 hours, remove from the oven and allow to cool fully.

5. Once the squash is cool, scrape the flesh out of the skin, including the darkened caramelized bits. Place the cooked squash, cooked pears, olive oil, cinnamon, and sea salt into a food processor and pulse until smooth. This puree will keep in an airtight container in the refrigerator for up to 1 week.

SERVES 8
PER SERVING: calories 152, fat 5 g, protein 2 g, carbohydrates 28 g, dietary fiber 5 g

crunchy maple-walnut popcorn

This sweet and crunchy snack is a great alternative to the famous boxed treat that comes with a little prize inside. If nut allergies are an issue, skip the walnuts and let the maple crunch all on its own.

ingredients

¼ **cup butter or soy-free, nonhydrogenated margarine, plus more for coating the bowl**

½ **cup popcorn kernels**

½ **cup walnut pieces, toasted**

1 **cup pure maple syrup**

½ **teaspoon salt**

SERVES 8

PER SERVING: calories 195, fat 6 g, protein 1 g, carbohydrates 33 g, dietary fiber 1 g

PREP TIME: 20 minutes
COOK TIME: 20 minutes

1. Lightly coat a large bowl with butter or margarine. Line a rimmed baking sheet with parchment paper.

2. Pop the popcorn either on the stovetop or in an air popper. Follow the instructions on the package, but do not use microwave popcorn. Place the popped corn in the prepared bowl, and sprinkle the toasted walnut pieces on top.

3. In a medium saucepan, over medium heat, gently melt the butter. Add the maple syrup and salt, turn the heat to medium-high, and bring the mixture to a boil. Reduce the heat and cook at a low boil for 12 to 15 minutes, until the mixture reaches 300°F on a candy thermometer.

4. Working quickly, pour the maple syrup over the popcorn and walnuts, tossing to coat completely.

5. Spread the popcorn onto the prepared baking sheet. When cool, break apart. Store in an airtight container for up to 5 days.

easy ways to make any snack special

Kids tend to get a lot of their daily calories from snacks—so it makes sense to serve them fresh, healthy fare that'll load them up with the vitamins and minerals they need (instead of the sugar they don't). But plain old apple slices or carrot sticks become less-than-appealing when your child sees Jimmy from down the street munching on salty chips or neon-colored fruit snacks. Here are four ways to dress up the healthy stuff so your kid actually wants to eat it.

MAKE "FRIES" Chefs might call them oven-roasted vegetables, but we call them oven-fries—a name that's instantly appealing to kids. Slice sturdy veggies like sweet potatoes, carrots, parsnips, or squash in thin strips, toss with olive oil, and roast at 400°F until crispy.

DO THE DIP You wouldn't eat a salad without dressing, so why expect your kid to eat raw veggies (or fruit) without dip? Dunk broccoli florets or pepper strips in hummus, sunflower seed butter sauce, or ranch dressing; dip apple, pear, or banana slices in yogurt sweetened with honey.

MAKE A FACE You've probably seen recipes for those cute, clever—and complicated—treats shaped like sailboats or circus tents. If you don't have the time or the crafting skills to make those happen, there is one surefire shape you can do with almost any treat: a happy face. Whatever snack you're serving up, turn it into two eyes and a smile, and you're sure to get a grin from your kid, too.

STICK IT ON A STICK For whatever reason, kids go nuts for food on a stick. So put those kiwifruit slices or cherry tomatoes on a kebab—instant fun.

parties

EVER SEEN a kid with an allergy at a birthday party eating his wheat-free pretzels and sliced pear while everyone else gorges on pizza and cake? Let's not allow that to happen anymore! Birthday and other parties are major thrills in kids' lives, and those with food allergies deserve to have a good time. Hey, in some ways they deserve a *better* time, given how often they feel left out.

Fortunately, the recipes in this chapter will not only be a hit for a food-sensitive kid—every guest (and parents, too) will gobble them up. Whether you're serving up nutritious savory treats (like polenta pizzas or turkey sliders) or heading straight to the dairy-free cake (trust us, it's delicious), your party will be the talk of the block. Don't be surprised if the other parents come asking what the secret to your fudgy brownies is (hint: black beans). What a great way to introduce other families to the positive side of living with allergies.

These recipes are all easy to double or triple, depending on what kind of party you've taken on. Happy celebrating!

KEY

G=GLUTEN-FREE

D=DAIRY-FREE

N=NUT-FREE

E=EGG-FREE

S=SOY-FREE

1-2-3 Party Mix G, D, N, E, S 177

Animal Bagels G option, D option, N, E, S option 178

Carnival Corn Dogs G, D, N, E, S 179

Cool and Crunchy Summer Rolls G, D, N, E 180

Golden Gluten-Free Cupcakes G, D, N, S 182

Fudgy Chocolate Frosting G, D, N, S 184

**I-Can't-Believe-It's-Not-Buttercream
Chocolate Cake** D, N, E, S 185

Dairy-Free Vanilla Frosting G, D, N, E, S 186

Giant Cookie Cake G, D, N, E, S 189

Ice Cream Sandwiches for Everyone G, D, N, E, S 191

Double Chocolate Chunk Cookies G, D, N, E, S 192

Wholesome Vanilla Ice Cream G, D, N, E, S 193

Green Monster Dip with Carrot Coins G, D, N, E, S 194

Silly Monkey Bread D, N, E, S 196

Party-On Chili G, D, N, E, S 198

Sweet and Salty Popcorn Balls G option, D, N, E, S 199

Polenta Mini Pizzas G, N, E, S 201

South of the Border Sushi G, D, N, E, S 202

Sunny Candy Pops G, D, N, E, S 203

Cinnachips and Rainbow Salsa G, D, N, E, S 204

Black Bean Brownie Bites G, D, N, S 205

Teriyaki Turkey Sliders G option, D, N, E 206

Soft Pretzels with Honey Mustard Sauce D, N, E, S option . 208

Crispy Cheese Bites with Bean Salsa G, N, E, S option . . . 210

Caramelized Double-Onion Dip G, N, E 211

1-2-3 party mix

Popcorn and rice cereal make this party mix familiar, but easy-to-make pumpkin seed brittle makes for a treat that's extra special. Make the brittle up to two days in advance before tossing with the remaining ingredients at party time.

ingredients

Canola oil, for coating the baking sheet and spatula

1 **cup pumpkin seeds, toasted**

2 **cups raw cane sugar**

1 **cup water**

10 **cups salted popped popcorn**

5 **cups gluten-free rice square cereal**

SERVES 16

PER SERVING: calories 165, fat 1 g, protein 2 g, carbohydrates 38 gm dietary fiber 1 g

PREP TIME: 2 hours

1. Lightly coat a rimmed baking sheet and spatula with canola oil. Spread the pumpkin seeds in an even layer on the baking sheet.

2. In a medium stockpot over medium-high heat, add the sugar and water. Cook, without stirring, monitoring the temperature with a candy thermometer, for 5 to 7 minutes, until the mixture reaches 300°F.

3. Quickly and carefully pour the sugar mixture over the pumpkin seeds and spread evenly with the spatula. Set aside to cool for at least 1 hour, until rock-hard.

4. Using a rolling pin or meat pounder, crush the pumpkin seed brittle into very small pieces. Transfer the crushed brittle to a large bowl, and toss with the popcorn and rice cereal. Serve.

animal bagels

One easy way to get kids to gobble up veggies? Cover a bagel with a creamy spread and stick on the veggies in the shape of an animal face. For dairy allergies, use silken tofu; for soy allergies, use cream cheese.

ingredients

12 ounces firm silken tofu or softened cream cheese

¼ cup chopped fresh parsley

¼ cup chopped fresh dill

2 tablespoons olive oil

1 clove garlic

Juice of ½ lemon (omit if using cream cheese)

½ teaspoon salt

4 whole-wheat or gluten-free bagels, halved

16 pitted kalamata olives (about ¼ cup)

4 cherry tomatoes

1 small bunch chives

1 medium orange or yellow bell pepper

PREP TIME: 30 minutes

1. In a food processor, add the tofu, parsley, dill, olive oil, garlic, lemon, if using, and salt. Process to combine.

2. Spread the tofu mixture evenly on the 8 bagel halves.

3. For the eyes, slice 8 of the olives in half crosswise for 16 eyes. For the mouths, slice the remaining 8 olives in half lengthwise for 16 lips. For the noses, slice the cherry tomatoes in half for 8 noses. For the whiskers, slice the chives in half. For the ears, slice the bell pepper crosswise into 16 (½-inch) strips for 16 ears.

4. For each bagel, place 2 olive rounds for the eyes. Place a cherry tomato half in the bagel hole for the nose. Stick 3 chive halves on each side for the whiskers. Gently press a pepper strip on each side of the top of the bagel for the ears. Place two olive strips underneath each side of the cherry tomato for the mouth. Smile and serve!

MAKES 8 ANIMAL BAGELS
PER BAGEL (WITH TOFU): calories 173, fat 7 g, protein 8 g, carbohydrates 21 g, dietary fiber 3 g
PER BAGEL (WITH CREAM CHEESE): calories 299, fat 21 g, protein 8 g, carbohydrates 22 g, dietary fiber 3 g

carnival corn dogs

The gluten-free batter on these kid pleasers is satisfyingly doughy, and since they're baked, there's a lot less mess and fat. If you'd prefer a meatless version, swap out the hot dogs for veggie dogs. Please note that this recipe calls for potato starch, not potato flour.

ingredients

- ¼ cup canola oil, plus more for coating the pan
- 1¾ cups unsweetened rice milk
- ½ teaspoon apple cider vinegar
- 1¼ cups cornmeal
- ½ cup sorghum flour
- ¼ cup potato starch
- ¼ cup tapioca starch
- 2 tablespoons raw cane sugar
- 1 teaspoon baking powder
- ½ teaspoon xanthan gum
- ½ teaspoon salt
- ¼ teaspoon baking soda
- 12 all-natural hot dogs
- 12 bamboo skewers

PREP TIME: 10 minutes
BAKE TIME: 15 minutes

1. Preheat the oven to 425°F. Lightly coat two rimmed baking sheets with canola oil.

2. In a large measuring cup, combine the rice milk and vinegar. Stir and set aside.

3. In a medium bowl, add the cornmeal, sorghum flour, potato starch, tapioca starch, sugar, baking powder, xanthan gum, salt, and baking soda. Mix well to combine, then add the rice milk mixture and canola oil. Stir well.

4. Working quickly, dip each hot dog into the corn batter to coat completely and place on the prepared baking sheets. Bake for 14 to 16 minutes, until the batter is just beginning to brown.

5. Stick a bamboo skewer into the end of each corn dog and serve with your favorite condiments.

MAKES 12 CORN DOGS
PER CORN DOG: calories 296, fat 19 g, protein 7 g, carbohydrates 26 g, dietary fiber 1 g

cool and crunchy summer rolls

These refreshing, no-cook rolls are perfect finger food for a summer gathering. Save time by prepping the chopped veggies while the vermicelli noodles soak.

ingredients

DIPPING SAUCE

¾ **cup sunflower seed butter**

3 **tablespoons wheat-free tamari**

2 **tablespoons rice wine vinegar**

2 **cloves garlic, finely minced**

⅓ **cup warm water**

SUMMER ROLLS

9 **(8½-inch) rice paper wrappers**

1 **large cucumber, halved, seeded, and sliced into thin 2 to 3-inch strips**

1 **(7-ounce) package vermicelli noodles, prepared according to package directions**

2 **large carrots, peeled and grated**

18 **mint leaves**

PREP TIME: 20 minutes

1. To make the dipping sauce, combine the sunflower seed butter, tamari, rice wine vinegar, garlic, and water in a medium bowl. Whisk together and set aside.

2. To make the summer rolls, fill a wide (at least 12 inches) container with very warm water. Place one rice paper wrapper in the water for 15 to 30 seconds, or until soft and pliable.

3. Place the rice paper wrapper on a flat work surface in front of you. Place 3 to 4 cucumber spears in a bundle in the center of the wrapper. Add a small handful of the noodles next to the cucumber spears. Place a small handful of the grated carrots on top of the cucumber spears, then top the noodles with 2 mint leaves.

4. Roll the wrapper like a burrito (see Cooking with Kids, page 181). Place the seal side down. Repeat with the remaining wrappers and serve with the dipping sauce. Summer rolls will last 1 day in the refrigerator.

MAKES 9 ROLLS

PER ROLL: calories 250, fat 11 g, protein 8 g, carbohydrates 28 g, dietary fiber 4 g

COOKING WITH KIDS

teach your child to roll spring or summer rolls

STEP 1   Have your child place a rice paper wrapper in warm water and count to 20. If the wrapper has softened, she can take it out. If not, have her count to 10, check again, then remove the wrapper.

STEP 2   Place the wrapper on a flat work surface in front of her, then add the filling. Help her add the filling ingredients in a neat pile in the center of the wrapper to make the wrapper easier to roll up.

STEP 3   Take both sides of the rice paper wrapper and fold them over the filling. Then, she'll take the part of the wrapper farthest from her and fold that over the top of the two sides to tuck them in. Finally, she can roll the wrapper toward her to create a neat, wrapped package. Now the summer roll is ready to dip and eat!

golden gluten-free cupcakes

You just can't have a birthday party without a classic yellow birthday cake. Our moist cupcakes topped with smooth, fudgy chocolate frosting are really something to celebrate— even guests who don't need to eat gluten-free will be asking for these at their next party. Please note that this recipe calls for potato starch, not potato flour.

ingredients

2	**cups sorghum flour**
½	**cup potato starch**
½	**cup tapioca starch**
2	**teaspoons baking powder**
1½	**teaspoons xanthan gum**
1	**teaspoon salt**
1	**cup soy-free, nonhydrogenated margarine**
1½	**cups raw cane sugar**
2	**large eggs**
1	**cup unsweetened apple juice**
2	**teaspoons vanilla extract**
	Fudgy Chocolate Frosting (page 184)

MAKES 20 CUPCAKES

PER CUPCAKE: calories 343, fat 15 g, protein 3 g, carbohydrates 52 g, dietary fiber 2 g

PREP TIME: 20 minutes
BAKE TIME: 25 minutes

1. Preheat the oven to 350°F. Line 20 standard muffin cups with paper liners.

2. In a medium bowl, whisk the sorghum flour, potato starch, tapioca starch, baking powder, xanthan gum, and salt. Set aside.

3. In a large bowl or stand mixer fitted with the paddle attachment, beat the margarine for about 1 minute, or until fluffy. Add the sugar and beat for 2 minutes longer, until light and fluffy. Add the eggs, apple juice, and vanilla and beat until well-combined.

4. In batches, add the dry ingredients to the wet ingredients and beat until well-combined. Use a standard ice cream scoop to portion the batter into the paper liners. Bake for 20 to 25 minutes, until a toothpick inserted into the center comes out clean. Allow to cool completely before frosting.

5. Use a small spatula to spread frosting on each cupcake.

SUNNY CANDY POPS, PAGE 203

fudgy chocolate frosting

Thick, rich, and delectably sweet, this dairy-free spread is everything you'd expect of a chocolate frosting. Delicious on Golden Gluten-Free Cupcakes, Fudgy Chocolate Frosting also is a great topper for Butternut Blondies or (for true chocolate lovers) I-Can't-Believe-It's-Not-Buttercream Chocolate Cake.

ingredients

½ **cup soy-free, nonhydrogenated margarine, at room temperature**

3 **cups powdered sugar**

¼ **cup cocoa powder**

2 to 3 **tablespoons unsweetened rice milk**

1 **teaspoon vanilla extract**

In a large bowl or stand mixer fitted with the paddle attachment, beat the margarine until soft. Add the powdered sugar in batches, then add the cocoa powder, rice milk, and vanilla. Beat for 3 to 5 minutes, until light and fluffy. If not using right away, cover and refrigerate for up to 2 days. Allow to come back to room temperature before frosting.

SERVES 20

PER SERVING: calories 114, fat 5 g, protein 0 g, carbohydrates 19 g, dietary fiber 0 g

i-can't-believe-it's-not-buttercream chocolate cake

Yes, chocolate lovers: You can have a cake that doesn't need eggs but still tastes rich. Top it with Dairy-Free Vanilla Frosting for a perfect slice of cake that's sweet without being cloying. Or, for all-out chocolate decadence, use the Fudgy Chocolate Frosting (page 184).

ingredients

½ **cup canola oil, plus more for coating the pans**

1¾ **cups unsweetened rice milk**

1 **teaspoon apple cider vinegar**

1 **cup unbleached all-purpose flour**

¾ **cup whole-wheat pastry flour**

¾ **cup cocoa powder**

2 **teaspoons baking powder**

1 **teaspoon baking soda**

½ **teaspoon salt**

1½ **cups raw cane sugar**

¼ **cup brewed coffee**

1 **teaspoon vanilla extract**

Dairy-Free Vanilla Frosting (page 186)

SERVES 12

PER SERVING: calories 465, fat 18 g, protein 3 g, carbohydrates 78 g, dietary fiber 3 g

PREP + ASSEMBLY TIME: 20 minutes
BAKE TIME: 25 minutes

1. Preheat the oven to 350°F. Coat two 9-inch round cake pans with canola oil.

2. In a large measuring cup, combine the rice milk and vinegar and set aside.

3. In a medium bowl, add the all-purpose flour, pastry flour, cocoa powder, baking powder, baking soda, and salt. Whisk to combine.

4. In a large bowl, whisk the canola oil, sugar, coffee, and vanilla. Add the rice milk and mix well.

5. Working in batches, scoop the dry ingredients into the wet ingredients and stir to combine.

6. Divide the batter evenly between the prepared pans. Bake for 25 to 30 minutes, until a toothpick inserted into the center comes out clean. Cool completely on wire racks.

7. For each cake, run a butter knife around the edge of the cake to help loosen it from the pan, then place a plate on top and invert to remove from the pan.

8. To assemble, place one layer of the cake on a plate or cake plate. Frost with one-third of the frosting. Top with the second layer of the cake, and frost the top and sides with the remaining frosting. Refrigerate until 1 hour before serving.

dairy-free vanilla frosting

This classic vanilla frosting quickly will become a standard in your baking repertoire. For extra decorative fun, add a few drops of all-natural food coloring.

ingredients

½ **cup soy-free, nonhydrogenated margarine, at room temperature**

3¼ **cups powdered sugar**

3 **tablespoons rice milk**

1 **teaspoon vanilla extract**

In a large bowl or stand mixer fitted with the paddle attachment, beat the margarine until soft. Add the powdered sugar in batches, then add the rice milk and vanilla. Beat for 3 to 5 minutes, until light and fluffy. If not using right away, cover and refrigerate for up to 2 days. Allow to come back to room temperature before frosting.

SERVES 12

PER SERVING: calories 196, fat 8 g, protein 0 g, carbohydrates 33 g, dietary fiber 0 g

COOKING WITH KIDS

teach your child
to frost a layer cake

STEP 1   After the cake has cooled completely, your child can use a small spatula to spread a thin base layer of frosting across the top of one of the cake layers. This will keep the surface of the cake from crumbling into the rest of the frosting. Refrigerate to let the crumb coat set, for at least 30 minutes.

STEP 2   Using the same spatula, have your child place a big scoop of frosting on the center of the cake. He can move the spatula in small, circular motions to continue spreading the frosting across the top of the cake.

STEP 3   Place the second layer of the cake on top of the first layer. Repeat step one to spread a base layer on the top of the cake. Repeat step two to frost the top of the cake.

STEP 4   Have your child spread another thin base layer of frosting on the sides of the cake, then place a bigger scoop of frosting on the sides and use the spatula to spread the frosting across the sides. Refrigerate for 30 minutes.

STEP 5   Decorate the frosting with his choice of sprinkles, colored frosting, nuts or seeds, chocolate chips—get wild! Then the cake is ready to serve.

giant cookie cake

Forget those cookie cakes you get from the mall. This double-layer confection is tastier, healthier, and totally allergen-free. And what child or adult doesn't love a big giant cookie? Please note that this recipe calls for potato starch, not potato flour.

ingredients

Canola oil, for coating the pan

2 cups sorghum flour

½ cup tapioca starch

½ cup potato starch

2 teaspoons baking powder

1 teaspoon salt

1½ teaspoons xanthan gum

1 cup soy-free, nonhydrogenated margarine, at room temperature

1 cup packed dark brown sugar

½ cup raw cane sugar

¼ cup molasses

2 tablespoons ground flaxseed whisked with ¼ cup warm water

2 teaspoons vanilla extract

1 cup gluten-free, dairy-free, soy-free chocolate chips

PREP + ASSEMBLY TIME: 20 minutes
BAKE TIME: 30 minutes

1. Preheat the oven to 350°F. Thoroughly coat two 9-inch round cake pans with canola oil.

2. In a medium bowl, add the sorghum flour, tapioca starch, potato starch, baking powder, salt, and xanthan gum. Mix to combine.

3. In a large bowl or stand mixer fitted with the paddle attachment, beat the margarine for 1 to 2 minutes, until soft. Add the brown sugar and cane sugar, and beat for 1 to 2 minutes longer, until light and fluffy. Add the molasses, flaxseed mixture, and vanilla and beat again until well-mixed.

4. Working in batches, add the dry ingredients to the wet ingredients, mixing until well-combined. Fold in the chocolate chips.

5. Divide the batter evenly between the prepared pans, smoothing the tops with a spatula (the batter will be very sticky). Bake for 20 to 30 minutes, until the edges are golden-brown and a toothpick inserted into the center comes out clean. Cool completely on wire racks.

continued on page 190

**Dairy-Free Vanilla
Frosting (page 186)**

6.   For each cake, run a butter knife around the edge to help loosen it from the pan, then place a plate on top and invert to remove from the pan.

7.   To assemble, place one cake on a plate or cake plate, rounded side up. Frost with half of the frosting, then top with the remaining cake, rounded side up. Place the remaining frosting in a piping bag (or plastic resealable bag with the corner tip snipped off) to decorate the top of the cake. Refrigerate until 1 hour before serving.

SERVES 16

PER SERVING: calories 498,
fat 23 g, protein 2 g,
carbohydrates 81 g,
dietary fiber 3 g

ice cream sandwiches for everyone

These ice cream sandwiches are especially yummy made with Double Chocolate Chunk Cookies (page 192). You can also substitute Ginger Chip Drop Cookies (page 124); just double the recipe to make 40 cookies, or use your favorite allergy-free cookie.

ingredients

Double Chocolate Chunk Cookies (about 40 cookies) (page 192)

Wholesome Vanilla Ice Cream (page 193)

PREP TIME: 10 minutes
FREEZE TIME: 1 hour

1. Set out two rimmed baking sheets. Place 10 cookies face down on each baking sheet.

2. Top each cookie with a heaping spoonful of the ice cream, leaving a small border around the edge of each cookie uncovered.

3. Top each ice cream–covered cookie with a second cookie, face up, and freeze the cookies for at least 1 hour or overnight.

MAKES 20 ICE CREAM SANDWICHES
PER ICE CREAM SANDWICH:
calories 427, fat 20 g,
protein 2 g,
carbohydrates 65 g,
dietary fiber 3 g

GLUTEN-FREE

DAIRY-FREE

NUT-FREE

EGG-FREE

SOY-FREE

double chocolate chunk cookies

Whether eaten as part of an ice cream sandwich or on their own, these sandy cookies are a chocolate lover's dream. Warm them briefly in the toaster oven or microwave for an extra-gooey treat, if desired. Please note that this recipe calls for potato starch, not potato flour.

ingredients

PREP TIME: 10 minutes
BAKE TIME: 12 minutes

Canola oil, for coating the pan

1½ **cups sorghum flour**

½ **cup cocoa powder**

½ **cup tapioca starch**

½ **cup potato starch**

2 **teaspoons baking powder**

1½ **teaspoons xanthan gum**

1 **teaspoon salt**

½ **teaspoon baking soda**

1 **cup soy-free, nonhydrogenated margarine, at room temperature**

1½ **cups raw cane sugar**

¼ **cup molasses**

2 **tablespoons ground flaxseed whisked with ¼ cup warm water**

2 **teaspoons vanilla extract**

1½ **cups gluten-free, dairy-free, soy-free chocolate chips**

1. Preheat the oven to 350°F. Coat two rimmed baking sheets with canola oil.

2. In a medium bowl, add the sorghum flour, cocoa powder, tapioca starch, potato starch, baking powder, xanthan gum, salt, and baking soda. Mix well to combine.

3. In a bowl or stand mixer fitted with the paddle attachment, beat the margarine for about 30 seconds, until creamy. Add the sugar and beat again for 1 to 2 minutes, until light and fluffy. Add the molasses, flaxseed mixture, and vanilla, mixing well to combine.

4. Slowly add the dry ingredients to the wet ingredients, mixing well to combine. Fold in the chocolate chips.

5. Use a tablespoon to drop the dough onto the baking sheets. Bake for 12 to 14 minutes, until the cookies are just beginning to brown around the edges.

6. Let the cookies cool on the baking sheets for 3 to 5 minutes before transferring to a wire rack and allowing to cool completely.

MAKES 40 COOKIES
PER COOKIE: calories 139, fat 7 g, protein 1 g, carbohydrates 20 g, dietary fiber 1 g

wholesome
vanilla ice cream

Traditional ice cream gets its rich, creamy texture from a combination of cream and eggs. Who knew superhealthy ingredients such as bananas, tahini, and coconut milk could yield such a convincing substitute?

ingredients

- 1 **(15-ounce) can coconut milk (do not use light)**
- 1 **large banana, cut into chunks and frozen**
- 1 **cup raw cane sugar**
- ½ **cup tahini**
- ½ **cup unsweetened rice milk**
- ½ **cup tapioca starch**
- 1 **tablespoon vanilla extract**
- ¼ **teaspoon xanthan gum**
- ¼ **teaspoon salt**

PREP TIME: 10 minutes
FREEZE TIME: 1 hour

1. Combine all the ingredients in a food processor or blender and puree until completely smooth. Pour into your ice cream maker and process according to your manufacturer's directions.

2. When the ice cream is the consistency of soft serve, transfer to a container and freeze for about 1 hour. The consistency should be slightly thicker than soft serve but won't be as hard as conventional dairy ice cream.

SERVES 8
PER SERVING: calories 339, fat 20 g, protein 4 g, carbohydrates 42 g, dietary fiber 2 g

green monster dip with carrot coins

Sliced carrot coins and baby spinach leaves give basic hummus a vibrantly colored (and supernutritious) update that's extra fun to eat. For larger crowds, double the recipe and prepare in batches.

ingredients

1   **(15-ounce) can chickpeas, drained and rinsed**

2   **tablespoons tahini**

2   **tablespoons fresh lemon juice**

2   **tablespoons water**

1   **tablespoon olive oil**

1   **clove garlic**

½   **teaspoon salt**

4   **cups packed baby spinach**

4   **large carrots, peeled and sliced diagonally**

PREP TIME: 5 minutes

1.   Add the chickpeas, tahini, lemon juice, water, olive oil, garlic, and salt to a food processor and puree until smooth.

2.   Add the spinach, 1 cup at a time, and puree until smooth. Transfer the mixture to a bowl and serve alongside the carrots.

SERVES 8

PER SERVING: calories 120, fat 5 g, protein 4 g, carbohydrates 17 g, dietary fiber 4 g

silly monkey bread

Traditionally dairy-laden (and often studded with nuts), this sweet pull-apart bread is still deliciously addictive. Kids love the bready sweetness—it's not quite cake, not quite a dinner roll, but totally fun.

DAIRY-FREE

NUT-FREE

EGG-FREE

SOY-FREE

ingredients

- 2¼ teaspoons active dry yeast
- ½ cup warm water
- ¼ cup raw cane sugar, plus more as needed
- 4 cups unbleached all-purpose flour, plus more as needed
- 2 teaspoons salt
- 1 cup warm rice milk
- ¼ cup canola oil, plus more for coating a bowl and a pan
- ½ cup soy-free, nonhydrogenated margarine, melted
- 1¼ cups packed brown sugar
- 2 teaspoons ground cinnamon

PREP TIME: 20 minutes, plus 1 hour 45 minutes rise time
BAKE TIME: 30 minutes

1. In a small bowl, combine the yeast and water with a pinch of sugar. Set aside for 5 to 10 minutes, until small bubbles form at the surface and the mixture smells bready.

2. In a large bowl, add the sugar, flour, and salt. Whisk well to combine.

3. Add the yeast mixture, rice milk, and canola oil to the flour mixture and stir to form a dough. Knead on a floured surface, adding more flour as necessary, until the dough is smooth and barely sticky.

4. Coat a large bowl with canola oil, and place the dough inside. Cover with a kitchen towel and allow to rise in a warm place for about 1 hour, or until double in size.

5. Cover a surface or cutting board with parchment paper. Form the dough into golf ball–size balls (about 60 total), placing on the parchment. Allow to rise for 45 minutes longer, until double in size.

6. Preheat the oven to 350°F. Lightly coat a Bundt pan with canola oil.

7. Pour the melted margarine into a shallow bowl, and combine the brown sugar and cinnamon in a second shallow bowl.

8. Use one hand to dip each ball into the melted margarine, and the other hand to roll it in the brown sugar mixture. Place each ball in the Bundt pan to form three to four layers of dough balls.

9. Bake for 25 to 30 minutes, until the top of the monkey bread is golden-brown. Allow to cool completely before turning out onto a plate or cake plate. Serve.

SERVES 12
PER SERVING: calories 374, fat 13 g, protein 5 g, carbohydrates 69 g, dietary fiber 1 g

party-on chili

One fun way to feed a crowd is with a chili bar. Set out toppings like grated cheese, lettuce, diced avocado and tomato, sour cream, and salsa, and let your guests build their own custom bowls. Double the recipe for bigger parties.

ingredients

PREP TIME + COOK TIME: 30 minutes

2	tablespoons canola oil
1	medium yellow onion, diced
1	large green bell pepper, diced
1	large red bell pepper, diced
1	jalapeño pepper, seeded and diced
1	clove garlic, minced
2	teaspoons ground cumin
1	teaspoon chile powder
½	teaspoon smoked paprika
1	(28-ounce) can crushed tomatoes
1	cup vegetable broth
1	(15-ounce) can pinto beans, rinsed and drained
1	(15-ounce) can black beans, rinsed and drained
	Salt and freshly ground black pepper

1. In a large pot, heat the canola oil over medium-high heat. Add the onion and bell peppers and sauté for 5 to 7 minutes, until soft.

2. Add the jalapeño, garlic, cumin, chile powder, and paprika. Cook, stirring frequently, for 1 minute.

3. Add the tomatoes, vegetable broth, pinto beans, and black beans and season to taste with salt and pepper. Bring to a boil, then simmer for 15 to 20 minutes, until heated through and slightly thickened. Serve hot with a variety of toppings, like diced avocados and tomatoes, salsa, cheese, and lettuce.

SERVES 8

PER SERVING: calories 168, fat 4 g, protein 8 g, carbohydrates 28 g, dietary fiber 8 g

sweet and salty popcorn balls

Be sure to let your child watch when you add the baking soda to the sugar mixture—she'll love to see it bubble up!

ingredients

10 **cups salted popped popcorn**

2 **cups pretzels or gluten-free pretzels, broken into small pieces**

6 **tablespoons soy-free, nonhydrogenated margarine**

1 **cup raw cane sugar**

½ **cup honey**

½ **teaspoon baking soda**

½ **teaspoon salt**

Canola oil, for coating your hands

MAKES 16 POPCORN BALLS
PER POPCORN BALL:
calories 192, fat 5 g,
protein 2 g,
carbohydrates 36 g,
dietary fiber 1 g

PREP TIME: 20 minutes

1. Place the popcorn and pretzels in a large heatproof bowl. Toss to combine and set aside.

2. In a medium stockpot, melt the margarine over medium heat. Add the sugar and honey and cook, without stirring, to 300°F on a candy thermometer. Add the baking soda and salt, stir briefly, and pour the mixture over the popcorn. Gently toss to coat the popcorn completely.

3. Allow the coated popcorn to cool for 2 to 3 minutes, until just cool enough to touch. Using oiled hands, form 16 tennis ball–size balls. Popcorn balls will keep in an airtight container for up to 3 days.

polenta
mini pizzas

These little pizza rounds couldn't be simpler to make—and it's a good thing, because you might need to whip up some more. The polenta gives the pizzas a slight flavor of corn, which kids tend to like for its sweetness. You can add any of your guests' favorite toppings, like roasted veggies, fresh herbs, or pepperoni.

ingredients

Canola oil, for coating the pan

1 **(18-ounce) tube prepared polenta, sliced into 12 rounds**

¾ **cup Mighty Marinara Sauce (page 56) or your favorite tomato sauce**

¾ **cup grated mozzarella cheese**

¼ **cup grated Pecorino Romano cheese**

PREP TIME: 5 minutes
BAKE TIME: 12 minutes

1. Preheat the oven to 400°F. Lightly coat a rimmed baking sheet with canola oil.

2. Place the 12 polenta rounds on the prepared baking sheet. Top each with 1 scant tablespoon of marinara sauce, 1 tablespoon of the mozzarella cheese, and 1 teaspoon of the Pecorino Romano cheese.

3. Bake for 10 to 12 minutes, until the cheese is bubbly. Serve.

MAKES 12 MINI PIZZAS
PER MINI PIZZA: calories 66, fat 2 g, protein 3 g, carbohydrates 8 g, dietary fiber 1 g

south of the border sushi

These Tex-Mex bites taste like tacos but take the shape of sushi rolls. They're super easy to eat, too, and won't cause a mess at a party. For homemade tortilla chips, brush leftover tortilla pieces with canola oil and bake at 425°F for 10 to 15 minutes, until crisp.

ingredients

1   **avocado, pitted and peeled**

    Juice of ½ lime

    Salt

14 **(6-inch) corn tortillas**

1   **(16-ounce) can all-natural, soy-free, gluten-free refried beans**

½   **small head iceberg lettuce, shredded**

2   **Roma tomatoes, diced**

MAKES 42 PIECES
PER PIECE: calories 33, fat 1 g, protein 1 g, carbohydrates 6 g, dietary fiber 1 g

PREP TIME: 30 minutes

1. In a small bowl, mash the avocado, lime juice, and salt to taste. Set aside.

2. With a serrated knife, slice the round edges off each tortilla to form squares. Pile the squares on top of each other on a plate and cover with a damp paper towel. Microwave for 30 seconds.

3. Spread 1 heaping tablespoon of the refried beans on a tortilla square, covering the entire surface. Spread 1 teaspoon of the guacamole across the middle of the tortilla. Top with a small handful of lettuce and a few tomato pieces on top of the lettuce.

4. Practice rolling the tortilla, pressing the top forward to form a cylinder shape (the tortilla should stay on the outside, like the nori in traditional sushi). The refried beans at the edge of the tortilla will help it seal on the bottom. Use a serrated knife to slice the roll into 3 pieces, and place on a plate or platter seam side down. Repeat with the remaining tortillas and serve.

sunny candy pops

Lovers of a certain orange-wrapped peanut butter cup are sure to love these allergy-friendly chocolate candies. They are lip-smackingly creamy and rich, and the yellow sprinkles give them a festive touch.

ingredients

Canola oil, for coating the pan

½ cup sunflower seed butter

½ cup powdered sugar, sifted

½ cup gluten-free, dairy-free, soy-free chocolate chips

3 tablespoons all-natural yellow sprinkles

15 lollipop sticks

MAKES 15 POPS
PER POP: calories 121, fat 8 g, protein 2 g, carbohydrates 11 g, dietary fiber 1 g

PREP TIME: 20 minutes
CHILL TIME: 30 minutes

1. Lightly coat a rimmed baking sheet with canola oil.

2. In a medium bowl, mix the sunflower seed butter and the powdered sugar until well-combined. Drop generous teaspoons of the dough onto the prepared baking sheet and roll each one into a ball. Place a lollipop stick in the center of each ball.

3. Place the chocolate chips in a microwave-safe bowl and microwave, stirring once or twice, for 60 to 90 seconds, until melted.

4. Dip each ball into the melted chocolate, then coat with sprinkles and return to the baking sheet. Chill for at least 30 minutes, or until the chocolate has hardened. Refrigerate leftovers in an airtight container for up to 4 days.

cinnachips and rainbow salsa

Instead of salt on your tortilla chips, sprinkle them with cinnamon sugar, then dip in a quick homemade salsa made with winter fruits. Pulsing the salsa in the food processor turns it a pretty pink color and makes it easier to scoop, but if you prefer a chunkier salsa you can skip this step.

ingredients

PREP TIME: 20 minutes
COOK TIME: 10 minutes

RAINBOW SALSA

1   apple, diced (about 1 cup)

½   cup diced grapes

½   cup pomegranate seeds

1   teaspoon pure maple syrup

2 to 4 tablespoons fresh lime juice

CINNACHIPS

4   cups canola oil, for frying

1   cup sugar

1   teaspoon ground cinnamon

8   10-inch corn tortillas, cut into eighths

1. To make the salsa, combine the apple, grapes, pomegranate seeds, and maple syrup in a medium bowl. Season to taste with the lime juice. Place in a food processor and pulse 3 to 4 times. Transfer to a bowl and refrigerate until ready to serve.

2. To make cinnachips, heat the canola oil in a medium saucepan to 360°F. Combine the sugar and cinnamon in a large bowl. Add a handful of the tortillas to the saucepan and cook, stirring frequently with a metal spider or slotted spoon, for 1 minute. Drain on paper towels, then toss in the cinnamon sugar. Repeat with the remaining tortillas. Serve the chips warm with the fruit salsa.

SERVES 8
PER SERVING (8 pieces):
calories 286, fat 14 g,
protein 2 g,
carbohydrates 40 g,
dietary fiber 2 g

black bean brownie bites

These brownies are shockingly satisfying to a hungry sweet tooth. Fudgier than traditional brownies, they'll give kids the sweetness they're looking for along with a healthy dose of fiber and protein, thanks to the black beans.

ingredients

1 **(15-ounce) can black beans, drained and rinsed**

3 **large eggs**

2 **tablespoons canola oil**

½ **cup agave nectar**

¼ **cup evaporated cane sugar**

¾ **cup unsweetened cocoa powder**

1 **teaspoon vanilla extract**

½ **teaspoon baking powder**

½ **teaspoon salt**

½ **cup chopped pecans (optional)**

MAKES 9 BROWNIES

PER BROWNIE: calories 330, fat 11 g, protein 14 g, carbohydrates 50 g, dietary fiber 11 g

PREP TIME: 7 minutes
COOK TIME: 50 minutes

1. Preheat the oven to 350°F. Line an 8-inch square baking dish with parchment paper.

2. Pulse the beans in a blender until almost smooth. Add the eggs and pulse until the mixture forms a smooth paste.

3. Add the canola oil, agave, sugar, cocoa powder, vanilla, baking powder, and salt to the blender and puree until completely smooth, scraping down the sides of the carafe with a spatula as necessary. Transfer to a bowl and fold the pecans, if using, into the batter, but do not blend.

4. Pour the batter into the prepared baking dish and smooth the top with a spatula. Bake for 40 minutes, or until a toothpick inserted into the center comes out clean. Cool completely before slicing into 9 brownies.

teriyaki turkey sliders

These fun-size burgers are perfect for party guests. They're tasty and wholesome but leave room for cake. The tamari and ginger give them a nice extra kick that's appealing to kids and adults alike.

PREP TIME: 10 minutes
COOK TIME: 15 minutes

ingredients

1   **pound 93 percent lean ground turkey**

¼   **cup panko, fine dry bread crumbs, or gluten-free bread crumbs**

2   **tablespoons finely chopped scallions, white and green parts**

1   **tablespoon wheat-free tamari**

1   **clove garlic, minced**

1   **teaspoon minced fresh ginger, or ⅛ teaspoon ground ginger**

1   **tablespoon canola oil or sesame oil**

8   **whole-grain slider-size buns or gluten-free slider-size buns**

1.   In a large bowl, combine the ground turkey, bread crumbs, scallions, tamari, garlic, and ginger. Mix well. Shape into 8 small patties.

2.   Heat the canola oil in a large nonstick skillet over medium heat. Add the patties (in 2 batches, if necessary) and cook, turning once, for about 15 minutes total, until no longer pink. An instant-read thermometer should register 165°F when inserted into the patties. These also can be grilled. If grilling, brush the patties with sesame oil before placing on the grill.

3.   Place on cocktail buns and serve with condiments of your choice.

MAKES 8 SLIDERS

PER SLIDER: calories 250, fat 10 g, protein 19 g, carbohydrates 19 g, dietary fiber 1 g

soft pretzels with honey mustard sauce

Brushing the pretzels with butter or soy-free, nonhydrogenated margarine after they're cooked gives them a richer flavor that offers an especially nice, mellow balance to the zingy honey mustard sauce. You can make the pretzels any size—smaller ones can be even more fun for kids.

DAIRY-FREE

NUT-FREE

EGG-FREE

SOY-FREE OPTION

ingredients

Canola oil, for coating a bowl and baking sheets

1½ **cups warm water**

1 **tablespoon instant yeast**

¼ **cup packed dark brown sugar**

3½ **cups unbleached all-purpose flour**

HONEY MUSTARD SAUCE

1 **cup mayonnaise or vegan mayonnaise**

¼ **cup Dijon mustard**

¼ **cup honey**

PREP TIME: 15 minutes, plus 45 minutes for dough to rise
COOK TIME: 15 minutes

1. Coat a large bowl with canola oil. Combine the warm water, yeast, brown sugar, and flour in a stand mixer fitted with the dough hook. Mix on medium speed for about 1 minute, or until the dough clears the sides of the bowl and forms a smooth ball. Transfer the dough to the prepared bowl, cover, and place in a warm spot (like the back of the stove) for about 45 minutes, or until double in size.

2. While the dough is rising, prepare the sauce. Combine all the ingredients in a small bowl and whisk until smooth. Refrigerate until ready to serve.

3. Preheat the oven to 500°F. Coat two rimmed baking sheets with canola oil. Turn the dough out onto a clean surface and cut into 12 equal pieces. Roll each piece into a rope about 24 inches long and shape into a pretzel, gently pinching the dough where it touches so it holds its shape.

⅓ **cup baking soda**

6 **cups water**

   Coarse kosher salt

3 **tablespoons melted
   butter or soy-free,
   nonhydrogenated
   margarine**

4. Combine the baking soda and the 6 cups of water in a medium saucepan and bring to a boil. Drop each pretzel, one at a time, into the boiling water for 30 seconds, then remove and place on a prepared baking sheet. Sprinkle the pretzels with coarse salt.

5. Bake the pretzels for 8 to 10 minutes, until deep golden-brown. Brush immediately with melted butter and cool for 5 minutes. Serve with the sauce.

MAKES 12 PRETZELS
PER PRETZEL: calories 274,
fat 10 g, protein 5 g,
carbohydrates 42 g,
dietary fiber 1 g

crispy cheese bites with bean salsa

These cheese crackers can be made using large presliced squares, or small slice-your-own pieces from a stick of cheese. Either way, be sure to use real full-fat cheese and not processed cheese. It's not only tastier—it bakes better! Topping them with the white-bean salsa makes for delicious chip-less nachos.

ingredients

½ **pound semihard cheese, like Monterey Jack, cheddar, or provolone, sliced ⅛ inch thick**

1 **(15-ounce) can cannellini beans, drained and rinsed**

⅓ **cup diced white onion**

2 **tablespoons chopped fresh cilantro**

Pinch of sea salt

PREP TIME: 2 minutes
COOK TIME: 10 to 15 minutes

1. Preheat the oven to 350°F. Line a rimmed baking sheet with parchment paper.

2. Place the cheese slices on the baking sheet at least 1 inch apart.

3. Bake for 10 to 15 minutes, until the cheese is golden-brown all over with crispy edges.

4. While the cheese is baking, stir together the beans, onion, cilantro, and salt in a medium bowl.

5. Using a spatula, transfer the crackers to a few layers of paper towels to absorb the excess fat. Allow the crackers to cool before topping with the bean salsa.

SERVES 6
PER SERVING: calories 235, fat 13 g, protein 15 g, carbohydrates 16 g, dietary fiber 4 g

caramelized double-onion dip

You'll never eat French onion dip from a packet again once you try this homemade version. Dicing the onions into small pieces allows for a quicker cooking time for caramelization. Serve with all-natural, kettle-style potato chips or chopped veggies like cucumbers, carrots, and celery.

ingredients

- 2 **tablespoons canola oil**
- 3 **cups chopped yellow onions (about 2 medium onions)**
- 2 **tablespoons butter, cut into pieces**
- ½ **teaspoon salt**
- 2 **tablespoons vegan mayonnaise**
- 2 **tablespoons sour cream**
- 1 **tablespoon heavy cream**
- 1 **teaspoon honey**
- 1 **teaspoon fresh lemon juice**
- 2 **scallions, white and green parts, chopped**

PREP TIME: 15 minutes
COOK TIME: 30 minutes, plus 3 to 4 hours chill

1. In a large sauté pan, heat the canola oil over medium-high heat. Add the onions, coating with the oil. Decrease the heat to medium, and cook the onions for 15 minutes, stirring every couple of minutes. Decrease the heat if the onions are turning black instead of golden-brown.

2. Add the butter, stirring to incorporate into the onions. Cook for about 10 minutes longer, or until the onions are caramelized.

3. Add the salt, mayonnaise, sour cream, and heavy cream and stir to combine.

4. Remove the onion mixture from the heat, and transfer to a small bowl. Stir in the honey, lemon juice, and scallions. Taste, and adjust the seasonings, if needed.

5. Cover and refrigerate for 3 to 4 hours, until cool. Serve with chips or veggies.

SERVES 6
PER SERVING: calories 140, fat 12 g, protein 1 g, carbohydrates 8 g, dietary fiber 1 g

fun with food party activities

Hosting a party at home and grasping for ideas to keep ten kids entertained for an afternoon? These old-fashioned games and activities will keep guests happy—and all your supplies are right in the kitchen!

BOBBING FOR APPLES The classic autumn game is just as fun today—and tastier, too, with so many varieties of the fruit available.

MAKE YOUR OWN _____ sundae, cupcake, chili bowl, pizza . . . the possibilities are endless. Mix meal time with craft time by giving each child a blank canvas (a scoop of vanilla ice cream, personal pizza crust, sandwich makings) and setting out a topping bar.

HOT POTATO DANCE Like regular hot potato, but more active. Have guests stand in a circle and dance while they pass along the hot potato. When the music stops, everyone must freeze—and the potato holder is out!

EGG SPOON RELAY See which guest can make it across the yard and back the fastest while balancing an egg on a spoon. You can minimize potential messes by hard boiling the eggs first—just don't tell the kids!

GUESS HOW MANY Fill a large jar with your child's favorite small candy or snack (like mini pretzels or sunflower seeds). Invite each guest to guess how many items are in the jar, then give the jar to whoever guesses the closest.

building a natural, allergy-free pantry

FOR BUSY families, a well-stocked pantry is key for quick meals, snacks, and treats. And since allergy-free replicas of standard kid favorites often require a few special ingredients, a cupboard that's always full of the specific items *your* family needs means your child can enjoy the fare she loves anytime. We try to buy products labeled with the USDA Organic seal whenever possible; though "natural" isn't a regulated term, the brands here are ones we trust to live up to their claims. Here, the stuff we always have on hand when cooking allergy-free eats:

beans, grains, and pastas

BEANS AND LEGUMES

High in protein, fiber, and complex carbohydrates, beans are a tasty and inexpensive way to make any meal filling and nutritious. Once drained and rinsed, canned beans are ready to eat in soups, salads, stir-frys, and dips. Organic brands include Eden, Amy's, and Whole Foods 365. Dried beans—which can be found in the bulk section of natural-food stores—require an overnight soak plus a few hours' cooking time, but tend to taste fresher and retain a firmer texture.

BLACK BEANS

When paired with avocado, antioxidant-rich black beans add staying power to breakfast tacos and baked sweet potatoes.

CHICKPEAS (GARBANZO BEANS)

Enjoy them in hummus, pasta dishes, or roasted in a hot oven for a high-protein snack.

FRENCH LENTILS

Sometimes called Puy lentils, this variety has a firmer texture and quicker cooking time (about 25 minutes versus 45) than conventional green lentils.

KIDNEY BEANS

Throw these all-purpose beans into soups, salads, and curries.

PINTO BEANS

A creamy bean, pintos pair naturally with sweet, barbecue-style sauces or Southwestern flavors.

GRAINS
BROWN RICE
Brown rice is a high-fiber, gluten-free grain that comes in multiple varieties. Stock your pantry with all-purpose medium- or long-grain rice, both of which work well in most casseroles, pilafs, or as a plain side dish. Choose the chewy, starchier short-grain rice for Asian dishes, and brown basmati rice to serve under Indian-style curries. Look for Lotus Foods, Lundberg Farms, and Rice Select.

GLUTEN-FREE OATS
In most food manufacturing plants, oats share processing equipment with wheat. If gluten is a concern in your family, be sure to buy oats that are certified gluten-free, like those from Bob's Red Mill.

QUINOA
Technically a seed, gluten-free quinoa is rich in protein and fiber. Available in white, red, or black varieties (they all taste the same) from Ancient Harvest and Bob's Red Mill, be sure to rinse quinoa in a fine-mesh strainer to remove its bitter (but harmless) coating.

WHOLE-WHEAT COUSCOUS
Couscous looks like a grain but is actually a type of tiny, quick-cooking pasta. It's made from wheat and is unsuitable for gluten-free diets.

WHEAT PASTA
Whole-grain pasta retains the protein, fiber, and minerals that are lost when pasta is made from refined wheat, or semolina. Eden, Arrowhead Mills, Bionaturae, Hodgson Mill, and Trader Joe's offer organic whole-wheat pasta.

GLUTEN-FREE PASTAS
Gluten-free pastas, available from Tinkyada and Trader Joe's, among others, can be made from a variety of flours, yielding different tastes and textures. Experiment with some of the following varieties to see which one your family likes best:

BROWN RICE PASTA
CORN PASTA
QUINOA PASTA

fats

LIQUID
COLD-PRESSED OLIVE OIL
Olive oil is sensitive to high heat and is best in lower-temperature sautés (not stir-fries), in salads or dressings, and at the end of cooking (such as drizzling over a finished pasta dish). As such, seek out cold-pressed varieties, like those from Spectrum and Eden, which aren't subjected to high temperatures during the manufacturing process.

EXPELLER-PRESSED CANOLA OIL
A neutral-flavored, all-purpose oil that works well in savory dishes or baked goods (if substituting canola oil in a recipe that calls for butter or nonhydrogenated margarine, use ⅓ cup of oil for every ½ cup of butter or margarine). Expeller-pressed oil is made by crushing nuts or seeds; unlike conventional methods, it does not subject the oil to high heat or chemicals, which can damage the oil.

UNREFINED, EXPELLER-PRESSED TOASTED SESAME OIL

A drop is all you need to add an Asian flavor to stir-frys, dipping sauces, and more. We recommend the unrefined, expeller-pressed toasted sesame oil from Spectrum and Eden.

VIRGIN COCONUT OIL

The versatile fat is solid (often called coconut butter) when kept below 76 degrees; at higher temperatures, it melts into an oil. (Most brands are sold as solids in glass jars or plastic tubs, but are usually labeled as oils.) Use in place of butter or oil for a slightly sweet, tropical flavor.

SOLID

BUTTER

Butter made from organic milk is a good, all-natural choice for baking and some cooking in families without dairy allergies. Horizon, Nature's Promise, Trader Joe's, Whole Foods 365, O Organics, and Organic Valley are all good choices.

NONHYDROGENATED VEGETABLE SHORTENING

It's not something you'll use *too* often, but nonhydrogenated vegetable shortening, like that from Spectrum, helps keep dairy- and gluten-free pie crusts and other pastry doughs tender and flaky.

SOY-FREE, NONHYDROGENATED MARGARINE

Many conventional varieties contain trans-fat, giving the word "margarine" a bad rap. However, organic versions (like Earth Balance) of the dairy-free spread are made from heart-healthy, nonhydrogenated vegetable oils—and are trans fat–free.

flours and starches

FLOUR

WHOLE-WHEAT FLOUR

Flour that still contains the wheat's bran and germ, it offers more fiber, vitamins, and minerals than white flour. Use whole-wheat flour to enhance nutrition in yeast breads or fresh pasta dough, but avoid it in baked goods, where its coarser texture produces tough results.

WHOLE-WHEAT PASTRY FLOUR

A lighter, more finely ground variety of whole-wheat flour that's available at most natural-foods stores. It yields a similar texture in cookies, muffins, cakes, quick breads, pancakes, waffles, and other baked goods as white flour but offers more fiber and nutrients.

Look for organic brands of these flours, like Arrowhead Mills, Bob's Red Mill, Hodgson Mill, and King Arthur Flour.

GLUTEN-FREE FLOURS

BLANCHED ALMOND MEAL OR FLOUR

A rich, buttery flour made from finely ground almonds. Find it in natural-food stores or online (we like almond flour from Bob's Red Mill), and store in the freezer to prevent rancidity.

CHICKPEA FLOUR OR GARFAVA FLOUR

As the name implies, high-protein chickpea flour (sometimes called *besan*) is made entirely from ground chickpeas. Garfava flour is a mixture of ground chickpeas and fava beans, and can be used interchangeably with the chickpea-only variety. Both have a slightly beany taste, so they often work best in baking when paired with other, more neutral-tasting flours. For egg-free baking: 1 tablespoon of either flour mixed with 2 tablespoons of warm water can be substituted for 1 egg. The flours are available at many health food stores and Indian specialty stores.

CORNMEAL OR CORN FLOUR

Both add a slightly sweet flavor and crunchy texture to muffins, pancakes, and quick breads. Blue-colored varieties are higher in antioxidants than their white and yellow counterparts, but taste the same.

OAT FLOUR

Oat flour works well in muffins, cakes, quick breads, and cookies. When made at home by grinding oats in a food processor, the texture won't be as fine, so its best purchased from natural-food stores. Since some oats are processed in facilities that also process gluten, make sure your oat flour is certified gluten-free.

RICE FLOUR

When used in combination with other flours and starches, white rice flour adds a lighter texture to baked goods. Heartier brown rice flour has more fiber and nutrients, but its coarser texture can sometimes yield gritty results. Both are available in many natural-food stores; try varieties by Arrowhead Mills.

SORGHUM FLOUR

When combined with starches, sorghum flour's neutral flavor and fine consistency yields baked goods whose textures are similar to those made with wheat flour. Sorghum flour from Bob's Red Mill can be found in the gluten-free sections of many grocery stores.

STARCHES

CORNSTARCH

Use it as a thickener in sauces, or egg- and dairy-free versions of custard-type dishes like pudding or some pie fillings. Look for varieties that are certified organic and GMO-free.

POTATO STARCH

Up the moisture and lightness of baked goods with potato starch, which can be found in most grocery stores. Different than potato flour—which is baked, dried, and ground potatoes—potato starch is only the dried starch of the potato. The two cannot be used interchangeably.

TAPIOCA STARCH

Tapioca starch is ground from the root of the cassava plant, a tropical tuber. It lightens the texture of baked goods and creates crisp crusts in fried foods.

XANTHAN GUM

An essential ingredient in gluten-free baking made from fermented corn, xanthan gum works to bind and thicken gluten-free batters. A bag of xanthan gum can be pricey, but a little goes a long way—add ½ teaspoon per cup of gluten-free flour in yeast-free baked goods, and 1 teaspoon per cup of gluten-free flour in yeasted baked goods.

When searching for gluten-free flours, search for Bob's Red Mill, Arrowhead Mills, and Hodgson Mill.

fruits, nuts, and seeds

DRIED FRUITS
Sweet and chewy, with highly concentrated amounts of fiber, vitamins, and minerals, dried fruits are perfect for snacking or adding texture and flavor to a variety of dishes. Be sure to purchase natural, unsulphured varieties that are free of added sugar, which can be found in the bulk section of natural-food stores. Some of our favorites to keep on hand:

APPLES	DATES	PINEAPPLE
APRICOTS	FIGS	RAISINS
CRANBERRIES	MANGOES	

NUTS AND NUT BUTTERS
Chock-full of protein and healthy fats, nuts and nut butters add richness and body to a number of dishes (chopped and tossed into salads or pasta, or stirred into soups or sauces) and make for satisfying snacking. Look for organic nut butters, like those from Arrowhead Mills, Maranatha, O Organics, and Smuckers, or make your own by grinding nuts in a food processor.

SEEDS AND SEED BUTTERS
They serve the same purpose as nuts and nut butters but are safe for those with peanut and tree nut allergies.

FLAXSEEDS
Be sure to buy flaxseed meal. Flaxseeds are difficult to grind superfine at home, and the body can't absorb any of the nutrients from the whole seeds. Whisk 1 tablespoon ground flaxseed with 2 tablespoons warm water to replace 1 egg in baked goods.

PUMPKIN SEEDS
The bright green color is especially appealing to kids; you can make your own green pumpkin seed butter by grinding whole seeds in a food processor until a thick paste forms.

SESAME SEEDS AND TAHINI
If your grocery store's bulk section doesn't have sesame seeds, check the spice aisle, where they're usually sold in small spice jars. Tahini is a paste made from ground sesame seeds, similar to peanut butter or sunflower seed butter.

SUNFLOWER SEEDS AND SUNFLOWER SEED BUTTER
Sunflower seeds are an inexpensive source of protein, healthy fats, and vitamin E, and they add a welcome crunch to salads, trail mixes, and granolas. Sunflower seed butter, like SunButter, tastes remarkably similar to peanut butter.

spices, vinegars, and other flavorings

SPICES
You likely already have herbs and spices like basil, oregano, thyme, rosemary, cinnamon, cumin, and ginger on hand. Some additional flavors to consider stocking (Frontier and Simply Organic offer organic versions of all of these):

CHILE POWDER
Chile powders are the ground powders of dried chile peppers. They come in all spice levels, so experiment with different varieties to find one that suits your family's tastes. Use it in chili, taco filling, or anywhere else you want a Southwestern flavor.

SWEET SMOKED PAPRIKA

It adds a welcome smoky flavor to baked beans or other barbecue-style dishes—nixing the need for high-fat bacon. For maximum flavor, be sure to use within six months of buying.

TURMERIC

You won't taste a small amount of turmeric in most dishes, but it adds a yellow, eggy color to tofu-based scrambles and frittatas.

VINEGARS

APPLE CIDER VINEGAR

Add 1 teaspoon per cup of nondairy milk for a curdled effect that's similar to buttermilk. Try Bragg or Eden.

DISTILLED WHITE VINEGAR

An all-purpose vinegar (available from Spectrum) that adds tang to sauces and salad dressings.

RICE WINE VINEGAR

Keep on hand for Asian-style dipping sauces and stir-frys; one organic brand is Ka-Me.

UMEBOSHI PLUM VINEGAR

This salty, citrusy vinegar made from pickled Japanese plums imparts a cheesy flavor when used in certain dairy-free dishes. Usually used in tiny quantities, a small bottle should last most pantries a long time; try Eden Foods Ume Plum Vinegar.

KIWI recommends ORGANIC ingredients

OTHER FLAVORINGS

ALMOND EXTRACT

Most almond extract is not made from almonds; it's made using the oil from peach or apricot pits, which is listed as "bitter almond oil" or "oil of bitter almond" in the ingredients list. Still, check the label to make sure that the almond extract you buy also specifies nut-free. Look for Nielsen-Massey and Simply Organic.

NUTRITIONAL YEAST

High levels of B vitamins make nutritional yeast—a pale-yellow yeast that lends a cheesy flavor to dairy-free dishes—especially good for vegetarians and vegans, whose diets don't always include enough B vitamins. Look for Bob's Red Mill, or find it in the bulk section of a natural-food store.

WHEAT-FREE TAMARI

Traditional tamari is a type of soy sauce that's made without wheat, but the ingredient does lurk in some cheaper brands. Look for Eden or San-J, or check the label before buying.

sweeteners

GRANULATED
BROWN SUGAR
Brown sugar is white sugar with molasses. Seek out an organic and natural variety (like Wholesome Sweeteners or Florida Crystals), which is more likely to retain some of its original molasses and may contain trace nutrients. Most conventional varieties remove the molasses entirely and then add some back in. Making your own is easy, too: Add 1 to 2 teaspoons molasses to each cup of white sugar and mix well.

RAW CANE SUGAR
A variety of white sugar that's slightly more nutritious than conventional white sugar, raw cane sugar retains a bit of the original molasses and doesn't go through a chemical bleaching process. Organic, Fair Trade Certified varieties are best and can be found at natural-food stores.

LIQUID
AGAVE NECTAR
Agave nectar won't spike your blood sugar because it has a low glycemic index, making it a favorite among health-conscious eaters. However, some experts believe agave is more highly processed than other natural sweeteners and contains too-high levels of fructose, which can be difficult for the body to process. It's sweeter than sugar, so if you choose to use it, you can use less. When baking, add only half as much agave as you would sugar (adjusting other liquid volumes accordingly), and set the oven 25 degrees lower—the end result will be a product that tastes similar to one sweetened with sugar, but with a slightly more moist texture.

HONEY
Made by bees from flower nectar, honey is similar in sweetness to sugar. The raw, unprocessed stuff contains beneficial phytonutrients, and consuming local varieties may help alleviate seasonal allergy symptoms. Substitute it 1:1 for white sugar when baking, for a sweet, floral flavor, but lower the baking temperature by 25 degrees (since honey browns faster than sugar). Adjust moisture levels by reducing a recipe's liquids by ¼ cup for every cup of honey you swap in. Never give honey to a baby under 12 months old; in rare cases, it can cause infant botulism.

Wholesome Sweeteners and Madhava both offer organic honey and agave nectar.

MAPLE SYRUP
Not to be mistaken for pancake syrup, pure maple syrup comes from the sap of the maple tree. It can be substituted for sugar in baking just like honey (it'll boost the warm, homey flavor of baked goods with nuts or cinnamon). Plus the sticky stuff contains some immune-boosting zinc and manganese, and also boasts more than 20 health-boosting antioxidants, according to recent research.

MOLASSES
Molasses is what's left over when sugarcane is refined to make white sugar. It's a good source of calcium, iron, and potassium (especially the blackstrap variety). Molasses has an earthy, full-bodied taste that complements spiced or chocolaty baked goods—but doesn't quite work as a stand-alone replacement for sugar.

miscellaneous items

COCONUT MILK
Richer than other nondairy milks, coconut milk (like Ka-Me or Thai Kitchen) adds body and creaminess to nondairy soups, sauces, custards, and ice creams. Since it has a strong flavor, experiment to see whether you like the taste in different dishes.

OTHER NONDAIRY MILK
Options abound: Rice, almond, soy, hemp, or oat are all suitable replacements for cow's milk, depending on any other food allergies your family may have. Experiment with sweetened, unsweetened, or flavored varieties to find the one you like best. There are many brands available, including Trader Joe's, Whole Foods, Westsoy, and Organic Valley.

GLUTEN-FREE, DAIRY-FREE, SOY-FREE CHOCOLATE CHIPS
The semisweet chocolate chips are free of allergens and naturally sweetened with evaporated cane juice. Look for Enjoy Life.

SILKEN TOFU
Unlike Chinese-style tofu (the refrigerated blocks packed in water), silken tofu comes in aseptic containers that can be stored at room temperature. When blended, the bean curd forms a smooth, thick cream that successfully replaces eggs and dairy in custard-based desserts. One brand to try: Mori-nu.

UNSWEETENED APPLESAUCE
Swap no-sugar-added applesauce for some of the fat and/or sugar in baked goods or granola. It also makes a good egg replacer in cookies, muffins, and quick breads; combine ¼ cup applesauce with ½ teaspoon baking powder for each egg. Santa Cruz, Whole Foods 365, Vermont Organic are good organic options.

YELLOW MISO PASTE
A fermented soy paste, yellow miso's savory, salty flavor adds cheesiness to gluten-free dishes. Find it (try Eden) in the refrigerated section near the tofu.

private label brands

Living the "-free" life most definitely isn't free: Some of these ingredients cost more than their allergy-unfriendly counterparts, and organics can get pricey (getting the certification costs big bucks, and that gets passed on to you). However, major retailers' natural and organic store brands are a great option. Private-label products are required to meet the same organic certification standards as any other product (natural products are not regulated), and often name brands are the ones actually providing the store with the product. Because the store doesn't have to spend money on fancy labels and advertising like name brands do, the savings get passed on to you. Shop with confidence for organic store brands at Trader Joe's, Whole Foods, Wegman's, Stop and Shop (Nature's Promise Organic), Kroger (Private Selection Organic), and Safeway (O Organics).

For links to buy allergy-friendly products, plus even more recipes, visit allergyfriendlyfamilies.com.

metric conversions and equivalents

APPROXIMATE METRIC EQUIVALENTS

WEIGHT

¼ ounce	7 grams
½ ounce	14 grams
¾ ounce	21 grams
1 ounce	28 grams
1¼ ounces	35 grams
1½ ounces	42.5 grams
1⅔ ounces	45 grams
2 ounces	57 grams
3 ounces	85 grams
4 ounces (¼ pound)	113 grams
5 ounces	142 grams
6 ounces	170 grams
7 ounces	198 grams
8 ounces (½ pound)	227 grams
16 ounces (1 pound)	454 grams
35.25 ounces (2.2 pounds)	1 kilogram

VOLUME

¼ teaspoon	1 milliliter
½ teaspoon	2.5 milliliters
¾ teaspoon	4 milliliters
1 teaspoon	5 milliliters
1¼ teaspoons	6 milliliters
1½ teaspoons	7.5 milliliters
1¾ teaspoons	8.5 milliliters
2 teaspoons	10 milliliters
1 tablespoon (½ fluid ounce)	15 milliliters
2 tablespoons (1 fluid ounce)	30 milliliters
¼ cup	60 milliliters
⅓ cup	80 milliliters
½ cup (4 fluid ounces)	120 milliliters
⅔ cup	160 milliliters
¾ cup	180 milliliters
1 cup (8 fluid ounces)	240 milliliters
1¼ cups	300 milliliters
1½ cups (12 fluid ounces)	360 milliliters
1⅔ cups	400 milliliters
2 cups (1 pint)	460 milliliters
3 cups	700 milliliters
4 cups (1 quart)	.95 liter
1 quart plus ¼ cup	1 liter
4 quarts (1 gallon)	3.8 liters

LENGTH

⅛ inch	3 millimeters
¼ inch	6 millimeters
½ inch	1¼ centimeters
1 inch	2½ centimeters
2 inches	5 centimeters
2½ inches	6 centimeters
4 inches	10 centimeters
5 inches	13 centimeters
6 inches	15¼ centimeters
12 inches (1 foot)	30 centimeters

METRIC CONVERSION FORMULAS

TO CONVERT	MULTIPLY
Ounces to grams	Ounces by 28.35
Pounds to kilograms	Pounds by .454
Teaspoons to milliliters	Teaspoons by 4.93
Tablespoons to milliliters	Tablespoons by 14.79
Fluid ounces to milliliters	Fluid ounces by 29.57
Cups to milliliters	Cups by 236.59
Cups to liters	Cups by .236
Pints to liters	Pints by .473
Quarts to liters	Quarts by .946
Gallons to liters	Gallons by 3.785
Inches to centimeters	Inches by 2.54

OVEN TEMPERATURES

To convert Fahrenheit to Celsius, subtract 32 from Fahrenheit, multiply the result by 5, then divide by 9.

DESCRIPTION	FAHRENHEIT	CELSIUS	BRITISH GAS MARK
Very cool	200°	95°	0
Very cool	225°	110°	¼
Very cool	250°	120°	½
Cool	275°	135°	1
Cool	300°	150°	2
Warm	325°	165°	3
Moderate	350°	175°	4
Moderately hot	375°	190°	5
Fairly hot	400°	200°	6
Hot	425°	220°	7
Very hot	450°	230°	8
Very hot	475°	245°	9

COMMON INGREDIENTS AND THEIR APPROXIMATE EQUIVALENTS

1 cup uncooked rice = 225 grams

1 cup all-purpose flour = 140 grams

1 stick butter (4 ounces • ½ cup • 8 tablespoons) = 110 grams

1 cup butter (8 ounces • 2 sticks • 16 tablespoons) = 220 grams

1 cup brown sugar, firmly packed = 225 grams

1 cup granulated sugar = 200 grams

Information compiled from a variety of sources, including *Recipes into Type* by Joan Whitman and Dolores Simon (Newton, MA: Biscuit Books, 2000); *The New Food Lover's Companion* by Sharon Tyler Herbst (Hauppauge, NY: Barron's, 1995); and *Rosemary Brown's Big Kitchen Instruction Book* (Kansas City, MO: Andrews McMeel, 1998).

recipe index by allergen

gluten-free recipes:

BREAKFAST

Autumn Buckwheat and Flax Porridge, 15

Banana Bread Waffles, 5

Banana Chocolate Shakeroo, 34

Blueberry Corncakes, 6

Breakfast On-the-Go Tacos, 7

Brown Rice Breakfast Pudding, 8

Chickpea Soldier Dippers, 30

Farmhouse Buttermilk Biscuits and Gravy, 20–22

Frankenstein Sweet Potatoes, 26

French Toast Kebabs, 33

Fresh Almond or Rice Milk, 31

Gluten-Free Granola, 12

Green Eggs and Ham Breakfast Casserole, 9

Individual Egg-Free Frittatas, 13

Oaty Nut Crumble Sweet Potatoes, 25

Quinoa Maple Crunch, 14

Strawberry Rhubarb Muffins, 16–17

Sundaes for Breakfast, 28

Super Sweet Potatoes, 23

Tofu Scramble with Spinach, 19

Yogurt-Sesame Sweet Potatoes, 24

LUNCH

Almond Butter-n-Apple 'Wiches, 39

Barbecue Chicken Salad, 66–67

Butternut Squash and Zucchini Pancakes, 64–65

Cheddar Avocado Quesadilla, 41

Corn Chowder with Red Pepper Confetti, 45

Edamame Carrot Falafel Pitas, 43

Edamame, Carrots, and Shells, 57

Egg Salad and Ham Sandwich Sticks, 63

Eggplant, Tomato, and Mozzarella Circles, 44

Garden Wrap-n-Rolls, 58

Glazed Mini Meat Loaf Muffins, 60–61

Gluten-Free Pizza Dough, 48

Lemony Tuna Salad on Cucumber Slices, 70

Mighty Marinara Sauce, 56

No-Cream of Broccoli Soup, 40

Pizza Pockets, 47

Sweet Summer Corn Salad, 50

Tomato and Grilled Cheese Soup, 55

Veggie Bite Soup, 53

Veggie Sushi Bites, 68

World's Best Kale Salad, 46

DINNER

All-Day Roast Pork Shoulder, 104–5

Beef Satay with Peanut Noodles and Snow Peas, 98–99

Buddha Bowls, 80

Cheesy Stuffed Pizza Burgers, 102

Chicken Potpie with Sweet Potato Topping, 94–96

Cool Zucchini Noodles, 84

Corn Chip-Crusted Tofu Fingers, 82

Easy Lemon Chicken, 103

Franks-n-Beans, 81

Greener Sloppy Joes, 91

Healthy Turkey Stir-Fry with Broccoli and Cashews, 106

Lentil Burgers, 92

Olive Oil Twice-Baked Potatoes, 93

Spicy Mexican Shrimp Skewers, 101

Super Green Pesto Rice Bowl, 76

Tofu-Stuffed Shells, 75

Tuna-Brown Rice Bake, 97

DESSERT

Almond Flour Honey Cakes, 138

Almost-Raw Chocolate Cashew Fudge, 137

Cherry Chocolate Sorbet, 119

Chocolate Crumb Crust, 114

Chocolate Toasties, 111

Coconut No-Cream Pie, 113

Cozy Baked Apples, 120

Ginger Chip Drop Cookies, 124–25

Gluten-Free Pie Crust, 139

Mixed-Berry Fool, 121

No Moo Chocolate Pudding, 127

Nutty Fruit Pizza, 122

Raspberry Oat Bars, 129

Raw Summer Peach Tart, 134–35

Salted Caramel Hot Cocoa, 132

Spiced Pumpkin Pie, 140

Sunset Pops, 117

World's Simplest Soft Serve, 131

SNACKS

Apple Sun Smiles, 166

Buffalo Green Beans, 163

Chewy Strawberry Fruit Leather, 145

Chickpea Herb Crackers, 151

Chocolate Cinnamon Crisps, 165

Crunchy Maple-Walnut Popcorn, 172

Fruit and Nut Snackballs, 148

Fruity Guac, 168

Good-for-You Nachos, 155

Granola Squares, 152

Indoors S'mores, 167

Pear Dunkers with Cashew-Cinnamon
    Yogurt Sauce, 146

Pumpkin Mini Muffins, 153

Rice Ball Surprise, 160–61

Saucy Pears and Butternut Squash,
    170–71

Savory Roasted Chickpeas, 156

Spiced Carrot Fries, 158

Walnut-Stuffed Figs, 157

Zucchini Boats, 162

PARTIES

Animal Bagels, 178

Black Bean Brownie Bites, 205

Caramelized Double-Onion Dip, 211

Carnival Corn Dogs, 179

Cinnachips and Rainbow Salsa, 204

Cool and Crunchy Summer Rolls, 180

Crispy Cheese Bites with Bean Salsa, 210

Dairy-Free Vanilla Frosting, 186

Double Chocolate Chunk Cookies, 192

Fudgy Chocolate Frosting, 184

Giant Cookie Cake, 189–90

Golden Gluten-Free Cupcakes, 182

Green Monster Dip with Carrot Coins,
    194

Ice Cream Sandwiches for Everyone, 191

1-2-3 Party Mix, 177

Party-On Chili, 198

Polenta Mini Pizzas, 201

South of the Border Sushi, 202

Sunny Candy Pops, 203

Sweet and Salty Popcorn Balls, 199

Teriyaki Turkey Sliders, 206

Wholesome Vanilla Ice Cream, 193

dairy-free recipes:

BREAKFAST

Apple Cinnamon Swirl Bread, 3

Autumn Buckwheat and Flax Porridge,
    15

Banana Bread Waffles, 5

Banana Chocolate Shakeroo, 34

Blueberry Corncakes, 6

Breakfast On-the-Go Tacos, 7

Brown Rice Breakfast Pudding, 8

Carrot Cake Breakfast Cookies, 10

Chickpea Soldier Dippers, 30

Frankenstein Sweet Potatoes, 26

French Toast Kebabs, 33

Fresh Almond or Rice Milk, 31

Gluten-Free Granola, 12

Green Eggs and Ham Breakfast
    Casserole, 9

Individual Egg-Free Frittatas, 13

Oaty Nut Crumble Sweet Potatoes, 25

Quinoa Maple Crunch, 14

Strawberry Rhubarb Muffins, 16–17

Sundaes for Breakfast, 28

Super Sweet Potatoes, 23

Tofu Scramble with Spinach, 19

Yogurt-Sesame Sweet Potatoes, 24

LUNCH

Almond Butter-n-Apple 'Wiches, 39

Barbecue Chicken Salad, 66–67

Butternut Squash and Zucchini
    Pancakes, 64–65

Edamame Carrot Falafel Pitas, 43

Edamame, Carrots, and Shells, 57

Garden Wrap-n-Rolls, 58

Glazed Mini Meat Loaf Muffins, 60–61

Gluten-Free Pizza Dough, 48

Mighty Marinara Sauce, 56

No-Cream of Broccoli Soup, 40

Sweet Summer Corn Salad, 50

Veggie Bite Soup, 53

Veggie Sushi Bites, 68

World's Best Kale Salad, 46

DINNER

All-Day Roast Pork Shoulder, 104–5

Beef Satay with Peanut Noodles and
    Snow Peas, 98–99

Buddha Bowls, 80

Cheesy Stuffed Pizza Burgers, 102

Chicken Potpie with Sweet Potato
    Topping, 94–96

Cool Zucchini Noodles, 84

Easy Lemon Chicken, 103

Franks-n-Beans, 81

Greener Sloppy Joes, 91

Healthy Turkey Stir-Fry with Broccoli
    and Cashews, 106

Lentil Burgers, 92

Mac-n-Cheeze, 89

Olive Oil Twice-Baked Potatoes, 93

Southwest Beans and Corn Bread Bake,
    78–79

Spicy Mexican Shrimp Skewers, 101

Super Green Pesto Rice Bowl, 76

Sweet Potato Gnocchi with Lentils, 86–87

Tofu-Stuffed Shells, 75

DESSERT

Almond Flour Honey Cakes, 138

Almost-Raw Chocolate Cashew Fudge,
    137

Butternut Blondies, 116

Cherry Chocolate Sorbet, 119

Chocolate Crumb Crust, 114

Chocolate Toasties, 111

Coconut No-Cream Pie, 113

Cozy Baked Apples, 120

Ginger Chip Drop Cookies, 124–25

Gluten-Free Pie Crust, 139

No Moo Chocolate Pudding, 127

Nutty Fruit Pizza, 122

Raspberry Oat Bars, 129

Raw Summer Peach Tart, 134–35

Salted Caramel Hot Cocoa, 132

Spiced Pumpkin Pie, 140

Sunset Pops, 117

Whole-Wheat Lemon Shortbread, 130

World's Simplest Soft Serve, 131

SNACKS

Apple Sun Smiles, 166

Buffalo Green Beans, 163

Chewy Strawberry Fruit Leather, 145

Chickpea Herb Crackers, 151

Chocolate Cinnamon Crisps, 165

Crunchy Maple-Walnut Popcorn, 172

Fruit and Nut Snackballs, 148

Good-for-You Nachos, 155

Granola Squares, 152

Indoors S'mores, 167

Pear Dunkers with Cashew-Cinnamon
    Yogurt Sauce, 146

Pumpkin Mini Muffins, 153

Rice Ball Surprise, 160–61

Saucy Pears and Butternut Squash,
    170–71

Savory Roasted Chickpeas, 156

Spiced Carrot Fries, 158

Walnut-Stuffed Figs, 157

Zucchini Boats, 162

PARTIES

Animal Bagels, 178

Black Bean Brownie Bites, 205

Carnival Corn Dogs, 179

Cinnachips and Rainbow Salsa, 204

Cool and Crunchy Summer Rolls, 180

Dairy-Free Vanilla Frosting, 186

Double Chocolate Chunk Cookies, 192

Fudgy Chocolate Frosting, 184

Giant Cookie Cake, 189–90

Golden Gluten-Free Cupcakes, 182

Green Monster Dip with Carrot Coins,
    194

I-Can't-Believe-It's-Not-Buttercream
    Chocolate Cake, 185

Ice Cream Sandwiches for Everyone,
    191

1-2-3 Party Mix, 177

Party-On Chili, 198

Silly Monkey Bread, 196–97

Soft Pretzels with Honey Mustard Sauce,
    208–9

South of the Border Sushi, 202

Sunny Candy Pops, 203

Sweet and Salty Popcorn Balls, 199

Teriyaki Turkey Sliders, 206

Wholesome Vanilla Ice Cream, 193

nut-free recipes:

BREAKFAST

Apple Cinnamon Swirl Bread, 3

Banana Bread Waffles, 5

Banana Chocolate Shakeroo, 34

Blueberry Corncakes, 6

Breakfast On-the-Go Tacos, 7

Brown Rice Breakfast Pudding, 8

Carrot Cake Breakfast Cookies, 10

Chickpea Soldier Dippers, 30

Farmhouse Buttermilk Biscuits and
    Gravy, 20–22

Frankenstein Sweet Potatoes, 26

French Toast Kebabs, 33

Fresh Almond or Rice Milk, 31

Gluten-Free Granola, 12

Green Eggs and Ham Breakfast
    Casserole, 9

Individual Egg-Free Frittatas, 13

Oaty Nut Crumble Sweet Potatoes, 25

Quinoa Maple Crunch, 14

Sundaes for Breakfast, 28

Super Sweet Potatoes, 23

Tofu Scramble with Spinach, 19

Yogurt-Sesame Sweet Potatoes, 24

LUNCH

Barbecue Chicken Salad, 66–67

Butternut Squash and Zucchini
    Pancakes, 64–65

Cheddar Avocado Quesadilla, 41

Corn Chowder with Red Pepper Confetti,
    45

Edamame, Carrots, and Shells, 57

Egg Salad and Ham Sandwich Sticks, 63

Eggplant, Tomato, and Mozzarella
    Circles, 44

Garden Wrap-n-Rolls, 58

Glazed Mini Meat Loaf Muffins, 60–61

Gluten-Free Pizza Dough, 48

Lemony Tuna Salad on Cucumber Slices,
    70

Mighty Marinara Sauce, 56

No-Cream of Broccoli Soup, 40

Pizza Pockets, 47

Sweet Summer Corn Salad, 50

Tomato and Grilled Cheese Soup, 55

Veggie Bite Soup, 53

Veggie Sushi Bites, 68

World's Best Kale Salad, 46

DINNER

All-Day Roast Pork Shoulder, 104–5

Buddha Bowls, 80

Cheesy Stuffed Pizza Burgers, 102

Chicken Potpie with Sweet Potato
    Topping, 94–96

Cool Zucchini Noodles, 84

Corn Chip-Crusted Tofu Fingers, 82

Easy Lemon Chicken, 103

Franks-n-Beans, 81

Greener Sloppy Joes, 91

Lentil Burgers, 92

Mac-n-Cheeze, 89

Olive Oil Twice-Baked Potatoes, 93

Southwest Beans and Corn Bread Bake,
    78–79

Spicy Mexican Shrimp Skewers, 101

Sweet Potato Gnocchi with Lentils,
    86–87

Tofu-Stuffed Shells, 75

Tuna-Brown Rice Bake, 97

DESSERT

Butternut Blondies, 116

Cherry Chocolate Sorbet, 119

Chocolate Crumb Crust, 114

Chocolate Toasties, 111

Coconut No-Cream Pie, 113

Cozy Baked Apples, 120

Ginger Chip Drop Cookies, 124–25

Gluten-Free Pie Crust, 139

Mixed-Berry Fool, 121

No Moo Chocolate Pudding, 127

Raspberry Oat Bars, 129

Salted Caramel Hot Cocoa, 132

Spiced Pumpkin Pie, 140

Sunset Pops, 117

Whole-Wheat Lemon Shortbread, 130

World's Simplest Soft Serve, 131

SNACKS

Apple Sun Smiles, 166

Buffalo Green Beans, 163

Chewy Strawberry Fruit Leather, 145

Chickpea Herb Crackers, 151

Chocolate Cinnamon Crisps, 165

Fruity Guac, 168

Good-for-You Nachos, 155

Granola Squares, 152

Indoors S'mores, 167

Pumpkin Mini Muffins, 153

Rice Ball Surprise, 160–61

Saucy Pears and Butternut Squash,
    170–71

Savory Roasted Chickpeas, 156

Spiced Carrot Fries, 158

Zucchini Boats, 162

PARTIES

Animal Bagels, 178

Black Bean Brownie Bites, 205

Caramelized Double-Onion Dip, 211

Carnival Corn Dogs, 179

Cinnachips and Rainbow Salsa, 204

Cool and Crunchy Summer Rolls, 180

Crispy Cheese Bites with Bean Salsa, 210

Dairy-Free Vanilla Frosting, 186

Double Chocolate Chunk Cookies, 192

Fudgy Chocolate Frosting, 184

Giant Cookie Cake, 189–90

Golden Gluten-Free Cupcakes, 182

Green Monster Dip with Carrot Coins,
    194

I-Can't-Believe-It's-Not-Buttercream
    Chocolate Cake, 185

Ice Cream Sandwiches for Everyone, 191

1-2-3 Party Mix, 177

Party-On Chili, 198

Polenta Mini Pizzas, 201

Silly Monkey Bread, 196–97

Soft Pretzels with Honey Mustard Sauce,
    208–9

South of the Border Sushi, 202

Sunny Candy Pops, 203

Sweet and Salty Popcorn Balls, 199

Teriyaki Turkey Sliders, 206

Wholesome Vanilla Ice Cream, 193

egg-free recipes:

BREAKFAST

Apple Cinnamon Swirl Bread, 3

Autumn Buckwheat and Flax Porridge,
    15

Banana Bread Waffles, 5

Banana Chocolate Shakeroo, 34

Blueberry Corncakes, 6

Breakfast On-the-Go Tacos, 7

Brown Rice Breakfast Pudding, 8

Carrot Cake Breakfast Cookies, 10

Frankenstein Sweet Potatoes, 26

French Toast Kebabs, 33

Fresh Almond or Rice Milk, 31

Gluten-Free Granola, 12

Individual Egg-Free Frittatas, 13

Oaty Nut Crumble Sweet Potatoes, 25

Quinoa Maple Crunch, 14

Sundaes for Breakfast, 28

Super Sweet Potatoes, 23

Tofu Scramble with Spinach, 19

Yogurt-Sesame Sweet Potatoes, 24

LUNCH

Almond Butter-n-Apple 'Wiches, 39

Barbecue Chicken Salad, 66–67

Cheddar Avocado Quesadilla, 41

Corn Chowder with Red Pepper Confetti,
    45

Edamame Carrot Falafel Pitas, 43

Edamame, Carrots, and Shells, 57

Eggplant, Tomato, and Mozzarella
    Circles, 44

Garden Wrap-n-Rolls, 58

Gluten-Free Pizza Dough, 48

Lemony Tuna Salad on Cucumber Slices,
    70

Mighty Marinara Sauce, 56

No-Cream of Broccoli Soup, 40

Pizza Pockets, 47

Sweet Summer Corn Salad, 50

Tomato and Grilled Cheese Soup, 55

Veggie Bite Soup, 53

Veggie Sushi Bites, 68

World's Best Kale Salad, 46

DINNER

All-Day Roast Pork Shoulder, 104–5

Beef Satay with Peanut Noodles and
    Snow Peas, 98–99

Buddha Bowls, 80

Cheesy Stuffed Pizza Burgers, 102

Cool Zucchini Noodles, 84

Easy Lemon Chicken, 103

Franks-n-Beans, 81

Greener Sloppy Joes, 91

Healthy Turkey Stir-Fry with Broccoli
    and Cashews, 106

Lentil Burgers, 92

Mac-n-Cheeze, 89

Olive Oil Twice-Baked Potatoes, 93

Southwest Beans and Corn Bread Bake,
    78–79

Spicy Mexican Shrimp Skewers, 101

Super Green Pesto Rice Bowl, 76

Sweet Potato Gnocchi with Lentils,
    86–87

Tofu-Stuffed Shells, 75

Tuna-Brown Rice Bake, 97

DESSERT

Butternut Blondies, 116

Cherry Chocolate Sorbet, 119

Chocolate Crumb Crust, 114

Chocolate Toasties, 111

Coconut No-Cream Pie, 113

Cozy Baked Apples, 120

Ginger Chip Drop Cookies, 124–25

Gluten-Free Pie Crust, 139

Mixed-Berry Fool, 121

No Moo Chocolate Pudding, 127

Raspberry Oat Bars, 129

Raw Summer Peach Tart, 134–35

Salted Caramel Hot Cocoa, 132

Spiced Pumpkin Pie, 140

Sunset Pops, 117

Whole-Wheat Lemon Shortbread, 130

World's Simplest Soft Serve, 131

SNACKS

Apple Sun Smiles, 166

Buffalo Green Beans, 163

Chewy Strawberry Fruit Leather, 145

Chickpea Herb Crackers, 151

Chocolate Cinnamon Crisps, 165

Crunchy Maple-Walnut Popcorn, 172

Fruit and Nut Snackballs, 148

Fruity Guac, 168

Good-for-You Nachos, 155

Granola Squares, 152

Indoors S'mores, 167

Pear Dunkers with Cashew-Cinnamon
    Yogurt Sauce, 146

Pumpkin Mini Muffins, 153

Rice Ball Surprise, 160–61

Saucy Pears and Butternut Squash, 170–71

Savory Roasted Chickpeas, 156

Spiced Carrot Fries, 158

Walnut-Stuffed Figs, 157

Zucchini Boats, 162

PARTIES

Animal Bagels, 178

Caramelized Double-Onion Dip, 211

Carnival Corn Dogs, 179

Cinnachips and Rainbow Salsa, 204

Cool and Crunchy Summer Rolls, 180

Crispy Cheese Bites with Bean Salsa, 210

Dairy-Free Vanilla Frosting, 186

Double Chocolate Chunk Cookies, 192

Giant Cookie Cake, 189–90

Green Monster Dip with Carrot Coins,
    194

I-Can't-Believe-It's-Not-Buttercream
    Chocolate Cake, 185

Ice Cream Sandwiches for Everyone, 191

1-2-3 Party Mix, 177

Party-On Chili, 198

Polenta Mini Pizzas, 201

Silly Monkey Bread, 196–97

Soft Pretzels with Honey Mustard Sauce,
    208–9

South of the Border Sushi, 202

Sunny Candy Pops, 203

Sweet and Salty Popcorn Balls, 199

Teriyaki Turkey Sliders, 206

Wholesome Vanilla Ice Cream, 193

soy-free recipes:

BREAKFAST

Apple Cinnamon Swirl Bread, 3

Autumn Buckwheat and Flax Porridge,
    15

Banana Bread Waffles, 5

Banana Chocolate Shakeroo, 34

Blueberry Corncakes, 6

Breakfast On-the-Go Tacos, 7

Brown Rice Breakfast Pudding, 8

Carrot Cake Breakfast Cookies, 10

Chickpea Soldier Dippers, 30
Frankenstein Sweet Potatoes, 26
Fresh Almond or Rice Milk, 31
Gluten-Free Granola, 12
Oaty Nut Crumble Sweet Potatoes, 25
Quinoa Maple Crunch, 14
Strawberry Rhubarb Muffins, 16–17
Sundaes for Breakfast, 28
Super Sweet Potatoes, 23
Yogurt-Sesame Sweet Potatoes, 24

LUNCH

Almond Butter-n-Apple 'Wiches, 39
Butternut Squash and Zucchini
    Pancakes, 64–65
Cheddar Avocado Quesadilla, 41
Corn Chowder with Red Pepper Confetti,
    45
Egg Salad and Ham Sandwich Sticks, 63
Eggplant, Tomato, and Mozzarella
    Circles, 44
Garden Wrap-n-Rolls, 58
Glazed Mini Meat Loaf Muffins, 60–61
Gluten-Free Pizza Dough, 48
Lemony Tuna Salad on Cucumber Slices,
    70
Mighty Marinara Sauce, 56
No-Cream of Broccoli Soup, 40
Pizza Pockets, 47
Sweet Summer Corn Salad, 50
Tomato and Grilled Cheese Soup, 55
Veggie Bite Soup, 53

DINNER

Beef Satay with Peanut Noodles and
    Snow Peas, 98–99
Cheesy Stuffed Pizza Burgers, 102
Chicken Potpie with Sweet Potato
    Topping, 94–96
Cool Zucchini Noodles, 84

Easy Lemon Chicken, 103
Greener Sloppy Joes, 91
Lentil Burgers, 92
Mac-n-Cheeze, 89
Olive Oil Twice-Baked Potatoes, 93
Southwest Beans and Corn Bread Bake,
    78–79
Spicy Mexican Shrimp Skewers, 101
Super Green Pesto Rice Bowl, 76
Sweet Potato Gnocchi with Lentils,
    86–87
Tuna-Brown Rice Bake, 97

DESSERT

Almond Flour Honey Cakes, 138
Almost-Raw Chocolate Cashew Fudge,
    137
Butternut Blondies, 116
Cherry Chocolate Sorbet, 119
Chocolate Crumb Crust, 114
Chocolate Toasties, 111
Cozy Baked Apples, 120
Ginger Chip Drop Cookies, 124–25
Gluten-Free Pie Crust, 139
Mixed-Berry Fool, 121
Nutty Fruit Pizza, 122
Raspberry Oat Bars, 129
Raw Summer Peach Tart, 134–35
Sunset Pops, 117
Whole-Wheat Lemon Shortbread, 130
World's Simplest Soft Serve, 131

SNACKS

Apple Sun Smiles, 166
Buffalo Green Beans, 163
Chewy Strawberry Fruit Leather, 145
Chickpea Herb Crackers, 151
Chocolate Cinnamon Crisps, 165
Crunchy Maple-Walnut Popcorn, 172
Fruit and Nut Snackballs, 148

Fruity Guac, 168
Good-for-You Nachos, 155
Granola Squares, 152
Indoors S'mores, 167
Pear Dunkers with Cashew-Cinnamon
    Yogurt Sauce, 146
Pumpkin Mini Muffins, 153
Rice Ball Surprise, 160–61
Saucy Pears and Butternut Squash,
    170–71
Spiced Carrot Fries, 158
Walnut-Stuffed Figs, 157
Zucchini Boats, 162

PARTIES

Animal Bagels, 178
Black Bean Brownie Bites, 205
Carnival Corn Dogs, 179
Cinnachips and Rainbow Salsa, 204
Crispy Cheese Bites with Bean Salsa, 210
Dairy-Free Vanilla Frosting, 186
Double Chocolate Chunk Cookies, 192
Fudgy Chocolate Frosting, 184
Giant Cookie Cake, 189–90
Golden Gluten-Free Cupcakes, 182
Green Monster Dip with Carrot Coins,
    194
I-Can't-Believe-It's-Not-Buttercream
    Chocolate Cake, 185
Ice Cream Sandwiches for Everyone, 191
1-2-3 Party Mix, 177
Party-On Chili, 198
Polenta Mini Pizzas, 201
Silly Monkey Bread, 196–97
Soft Pretzels with Honey Mustard Sauce,
    208–9
South of the Border Sushi, 202
Sunny Candy Pops, 203
Sweet and Salty Popcorn Balls, 199
Wholesome Vanilla Ice Cream, 193

index

a

ADHD, xi

agave nectar, 220

All-Day Roast Pork Shoulder, 104–5

allergies. *See* food allergies; *specific allergens*

almond butter
  Almond Butter-n-Apple 'Wiches, 39
  Indoors S'mores, 167

almond extract, 219

almond flour, 216
  Almond Flour Honey Cakes, 138
  Nutty Fruit Pizza, 122
  Strawberry Rhubarb Muffins, 16–17

almonds
  cherry and almond granola, 12
  Fresh Almond Milk, 31
  Fruit and Nut Snackballs, 148
  Super Green Pesto Rice Bowl, 76

Almost-Raw Chocolate Cashew Fudge, 137

anaphylaxis, xiii

Animal Bagels, 178

apple cider vinegar, 219

apples
  Almond Butter-n-Apple 'Wiches, 39
  Apple Cinnamon Swirl Bread, 3
  Apple Sun Smiles, 166
  bobbing for, 212
  Cinnachips and Rainbow Salsa, 204
  Cozy Baked Apples, 120

applesauce, 221

artificial ingredients, xi

autism, xi

Autumn Buckwheat and Flax Porridge, 15

avocados
  Breakfast On-the-Go Tacos, 7
  Cheddar Avocado Quesadilla, 41
  Frankenstein Sweet Potatoes, 26
  Fruity Guac, 168
  Good-for-You Nachos, 155
  scooping, 154
  South of the Border Sushi, 202
  Sweet Summer Corn Salad, 50
  Veggie Sushi Bites, 68

b

bagels
  Animal Bagels, 178

bananas
  Banana Bread Waffles, 5
  Banana Chocolate Shakeroo, 34
  Fruity Guac, 168
  Sundaes for Breakfast, 28
  Wholesome Vanilla Ice Cream, 193
  World's Simplest Soft Serve, The, 131

Barbecue Chicken Salad, 66–67

bars and squares
  Black Bean Brownie Bites, 205
  Butternut Blondies, 116
  Granola Squares, 152
  Raspberry Oat Bars, 129

beans, 213
  Crispy Cheese Bites with Bean Salsa, 210
  Franks-n-Beans, 81

Good-for-You Nachos, 155

Party-On Chili, 198

South of the Border Sushi, 202

See also black beans; chickpeas; green beans

beef
  Beef Satay with Peanut Noodles and Snow Peas, 98–99
  Glazed Mini Meat Loaf Muffins, 60–61

bell peppers
  Buddha Bowls, 80
  Corn Chowder with Red Pepper Confetti, 45
  Garden Wrap-n-Rolls, 58
  Greener Sloppy Joes, 91
  Party-On Chili, 198
  potato-stuffed peppers, 107
  Southwest Beans and Corn Bread Bake, 78–79

berries
  Mixed-Berry Fool, 121
  See also blueberries; raspberries; strawberries

biscuits
  Farmhouse Buttermilk Biscuits and Gravy, 20–22

black beans, 213
  Black Bean Brownie Bites, 205
  Breakfast On-the-Go Tacos, 7
  Frankenstein Sweet Potatoes, 26
  Party-On Chili, 198
  Southwest Beans and Corn Bread Bake, 78–79
  Sweet Summer Corn Salad, 50

Blondies, Butternut, 116

blueberries

Blueberry Corncakes, 6

blueberry muffins, 17

Nutty Fruit Pizza, 122

bread

Apple Cinnamon Swirl Bread, 3

French Toast Kebabs, 33

Silly Monkey Bread, 196–97

Southwest Beans and Corn Bread Bake, 78–79

See also bagels; sandwiches

breakfast, 1–35

Apple Cinnamon Swirl Bread, 3

Autumn Buckwheat and Flax Porridge, 15

Banana Bread Waffles, 5

Banana Chocolate Shakeroo, 34

Blueberry Corncakes, 6

Breakfast On-the-Go Tacos, 7

Brown Rice Breakfast Pudding, 8

Carrot Cake Breakfast Cookies, 10

Chickpea Soldier Dippers, 30

Cozy Baked Apples, 120

Farmhouse Buttermilk Biscuits and Gravy, 20–22

Frankenstein Sweet Potatoes, 26

French Toast Kebabs, 33

Fresh Almond or Rice Milk, 31

Gluten-Free Granola, 12

Green Eggs and Ham Breakfast Casserole, 9

Individual Egg-Free Frittatas, 13

Oaty Nut Crumble Sweet Potatoes, 25

Quinoa Maple Crunch, 14

Strawberry Rhubarb Muffins, 16–17

Sundaes for Breakfast, 28

Super Sweet Potatoes, 23

Tofu Scramble with Spinach, 19

Yogurt-Sesame Sweet Potatoes, 24

broccoli

Buddha Bowls, 80

Healthy Turkey Stir-Fry with Broccoli and Cashews, 106

No-Cream of Broccoli Soup, 40

brown rice

Brown Rice Breakfast Pudding, 8

See also rice

brown sugar, 220

Brownie Bites, Black Bean, 205

buckwheat

Autumn Buckwheat and Flax Porridge, 15

Buddha Bowls, 80

Buffalo Green Beans, 163

bulgur, x

burgers

Cheesy Stuffed Pizza Burgers, 102

Lentil Burgers, 92

Teriyaki Turkey Sliders, 206

butter, 216

buttermilk

Farmhouse Buttermilk Biscuits and Gravy, 20–22

substitution, 219

butternut squash

Butternut Blondies, 116

Butternut Squash and Zucchini Pancakes, 64–65

Saucy Pears and Butternut Squash, 170–71

Super Green Pesto Rice Bowl, 76

C

cakes

Almond Flour Honey Cakes, 138

Dairy-Free Vanilla Frosting, 186

Fudgy Chocolate Frosting, 184

Giant Cookie Cake, 189–90

Golden Gluten-Free Cupcakes, 182

how to frost, 187

I-Can't-Believe-It's-Not-Buttercream Chocolate Cake, 185

canola oil, 215

caramel

Salted Caramel Hot Cocoa, 132

Caramelized Double-Onion Dip, 211

Carnival Corn Dogs, 179

carrots

Buddha Bowls, 80

Carrot Cake Breakfast Cookies, 10

Chicken Potpie with Sweet Potato Topping, 94–96

Cool and Crunchy Summer Rolls, 180

Easy Lemon Chicken, 103

Edamame Carrot Falafel Pitas, 43

Edamame, Carrots, and Shells, 57

Garden Wrap-n-Rolls, 58

Green Monster Dip with Carrot Coins, 194

Spiced Carrot Fries, 158

Veggie Sushi Bites, 68

World's Best Kale Salad, 46

casein-free diets

GFCF (gluten-free and casein-free) diets, xi

See also dairy-free *entries*

cashews and cashew butter

Almost-Raw Chocolate Cashew Fudge, 137

Healthy Turkey Stir-Fry with Broccoli and Cashews, 106

Pear Dunkers with Cashew-Cinnamon Yogurt Sauce, 146

Raw Summer Peach Tart, 134–35

casseroles

Chicken Potpie with Sweet Potato Topping, 94–96

Tuna-Brown Rice Bake, 97

cauliflower
Veggie Sushi Bites, 68
celiac disease, xiii
cereal
Autumn Buckwheat and Flax Porridge, 15
Gluten-Free Granola, 12
Quinoa Maple Crunch, 14
Cheddar Avocado Quesadilla, 41
cheese
Cheddar Avocado Quesadilla, 41
Cheesy Stuffed Pizza Burgers, 102
Crispy Cheese Bites with Bean Salsa, 210
Eggplant, Tomato, and Mozzarella Circles, 44
Mac-n-Cheeze, 89
Tomato and Grilled Cheese Soup, 55
Tuna-Brown Rice Bake, 97
Cherry Chocolate Sorbet, 119
Chewy Strawberry Fruit Leather, 145
chicken
Barbecue Chicken Salad, 66–67
Chicken Potpie with Sweet Potato Topping, 94–96
Easy Lemon Chicken, 103
white chicken chili, 107
chickpea flour, 216–17
Chickpea Herb Crackers, 151
Chickpea Soldier Dippers, 30
Gluten-Free Pizza Dough, 48
chickpeas, 213
Barbecue Chicken Salad, 66–67
Edamame Carrot Falafel Pitas, 43
Green Monster Dip with Carrot Coins, 194
Savory Roasted Chickpeas, 156
Zucchini Boats, 162
chile powder, 218

chili
Party-On Chili, 198
white chicken chili, 107
chocolate and chocolate chips, 221
Almost-Raw Chocolate Cashew Fudge, 137
Banana Chocolate Shakeroo, 34
Black Bean Brownie Bites, 205
Butternut Blondies, 116
Cherry Chocolate Sorbet, 119
chocolate chip muffins, 17
Chocolate Cinnamon Crisps, 165
Chocolate Crumb Crust, 114
Chocolate Toasties, 111
Double Chocolate Chunk Cookies, 192
Fudgy Chocolate Frosting, 184
Giant Cookie Cake, 189–90
Ginger Chip Drop Cookies, 124–25
I-Can't-Believe-It's-Not-Buttercream Chocolate Cake, 185
Indoors S'mores, 167
melting, 126
No Moo Chocolate Pudding, 127
Sunny Candy Pops, 203
Chowder, Corn, with Red Pepper Confetti, 45
cinnamon
Apple Cinnamon Swirl Bread, 3
Chocolate Cinnamon Crisps, 165
Cinnachips and Rainbow Salsa, 204
Pear Dunkers with Cashew-Cinnamon Yogurt Sauce, 146
cocoa
Salted Caramel Hot Cocoa, 132
See also chocolate
coconut and coconut milk, 221
Coconut No-Cream Pie, 113
Wholesome Vanilla Ice Cream, 193
coconut oil or butter, 216
conversions and equivalents, 224–25

cookies
Carrot Cake Breakfast Cookies, 10
Double Chocolate Chunk Cookies, 192
Giant Cookie Cake, 189–90
Ginger Chip Drop Cookies, 124–25
Whole-Wheat Lemon Shortbread, 130
See also bars and squares
Cool and Crunchy Summer Rolls, 180
Cool Zucchini Noodles, 84
corn
Barbecue Chicken Salad, 66–67
Corn Chowder with Red Pepper Confetti, 45
Southwest Beans and Corn Bread Bake, 78–79
Sweet Summer Corn Salad, 50
Corn Chip-Crusted Tofu Fingers, 82
corn flour, 217
cornmeal, 217
Blueberry Corncakes, 6
Butternut Squash and Zucchini Pancakes, 64–65
Carnival Corn Dogs, 179
Chickpea Herb Crackers, 151
Polenta Mini Pizzas, 201
Southwest Beans and Corn Bread Bake, 78–79
cornstarch, 217
couscous, whole-wheat, 215
Cozy Baked Apples, 120
crackers
Chickpea Herb Crackers, 151
Crispy Cheese Bites with Bean Salsa, 210
Crispy Cheese Bites with Bean Salsa, 210
cross-contact, x, xiv
Crumb Crust, Chocolate, 114
Crunchy Maple-Walnut Popcorn, 172
cucumber
Cool and Crunchy Summer Rolls, 180

Lemony Tuna Salad on Cucumber
  Slices, 70
Veggie Sushi Bites, 68
Cupcakes, Golden Gluten-Free, 182

d

dairy and dairy allergies, xiii, xiv
  GFCF diets, xi
  labeling rules, x
Dairy-Free Vanilla Frosting, 186
dates
  Fruit and Nut Snackballs, 148
  Raw Summer Peach Tart, 134–35
dessert, 109–41
  about sugar, 109, 141
  Almond Flour Honey Cakes, 138
  Almost-Raw Chocolate Cashew Fudge,
    137
  Butternut Blondies, 116
  Cherry Chocolate Sorbet, 119
  Chocolate Crumb Crust, 114
  Chocolate Toasties, 111
  Coconut No-Cream Pie, 113
  Cozy Baked Apples, 120
  Ginger Chip Drop Cookies, 124–25
  Gluten-Free Pie Crust, 139
  Mixed-Berry Fool, 121
  No Moo Chocolate Pudding, 127
  Nutty Fruit Pizza, 122
  Raspberry Oat Bars, 129
  Raw Summer Peach Tart, 134–35
  Salted Caramel Hot Cocoa, 132
  Spiced Pumpkin Pie, 140
  Sunset Pops, 117
  Whole-Wheat Lemon Shortbread, 130
  World's Simplest Soft Serve, The, 131
  See also parties
dinner, 73–107
  All-Day Roast Pork Shoulder, 104–5

Beef Satay with Peanut Noodles and
  Snow Peas, 98–99
Buddha Bowls, 80
Cheesy Stuffed Pizza Burgers, 102
Chicken Potpie with Sweet Potato
  Topping, 94–96
Cool Zucchini Noodles, 84
Corn Chip-Crusted Tofu Fingers, 82
Easy Lemon Chicken, 103
Franks-n-Beans, 81
Greener Sloppy Joes, 91
Healthy Turkey Stir-Fry with Broccoli
  and Cashews, 106
ideas for leftovers, 107
Lentil Burgers, 92
Mac-n-Cheeze, 89
Olive Oil Twice-Baked Potatoes, 93
Southwest Beans and Corn Bread Bake,
  78–79
Spicy Mexican Shrimp Skewers, 101
Super Green Pesto Rice Bowl, 76
Sweet Potato Gnocchi with Lentils,
  86–88
Tofu-Stuffed Shells, 75
Tuna-Brown Rice Bake, 97
dips, 173
  Caramelized Double-Onion Dip, 211
  Cinnachips and Rainbow Salsa, 204
  Fruity Guac, 168
  Green Monster Dip with Carrot Coins,
    194
  Pear Dunkers with Cashew-Cinnamon
    Yogurt Sauce, 146
  See also salsa
Double Chocolate Chunk Cookies, 192
Ice Cream Sandwiches for Everyone, 191
doughs
  Gluten-Free Pie Crust, 139
  Gluten-Free Pizza Dough, 48

dried fruit, 218
  Autumn Buckwheat and Flax Porridge,
    15
  Brown Rice Breakfast Pudding, 8
  Fruit and Nut Snackballs, 148
  Gluten-Free Granola, 12
  Granola Squares, 152
drinks
  Banana Chocolate Shakeroo, 34
  Salted Caramel Hot Cocoa, 132

e

Easy Lemon Chicken, 103
edamame
  Edamame Carrot Falafel Pitas, 43
  Edamame, Carrots, and Shells, 57
  Tuna-Brown Rice Bake, 97
egg allergies, xiii
Eggplant, Tomato, and Mozzarella
  Circles, 44
eggs, x, xiii
  Chickpea Soldier Dippers for, 30
  Egg Salad and Ham Sandwich Sticks, 63
  egg spoon relay, 212
  Green Eggs and Ham Breakfast
    Casserole, 9
  substitutions, 216–17
equivalents and conversions, 224–25

f

falafel
  Edamame Carrot Falafel Pitas, 43
FALCPA (Food Allergen Labeling and
  Consumer Protection Act), x
Farmhouse Buttermilk Biscuits and
  Gravy, 20–22
fava beans
  garfava flour, 64–65, 216–17

figs
  walnut and fig granola, 12
  Walnut-Stuffed Figs, 157
fish and fish allergies, xiii
  See also tuna
flaxseeds, 218
  Autumn Buckwheat and Flax Porridge,
    15
flours, 216–17
  gluten-free flour mix, 20
food additives, xi
Food Allergen Labeling and Consumer
    Protection Act (FALCPA), x
food allergies, ix–xi, xiii–xv
  allergy testing, xiii, xiv
  cross-contact, x, xiv
  desensitization, xiv
  emergency situations, xiii
  growing out of, xiii
  nutrition and, xiv
  susceptibility to, xv
  symptoms, ix–x, xiii
food dyes, xi
food labeling, x
Fool, Mixed-Berry, 121
Frankenstein Sweet Potatoes, 26
Franks-n-Beans, 81
French Toast Kebabs, 33
Fresh Almond or Rice Milk, 31
frittatas
  Individual Egg-Free Frittatas, 13
  pasta frittata, 107
frosting
  Dairy-Free Vanilla Frosting, 186
  Fudgy Chocolate Frosting, 184
frozen desserts
  Cherry Chocolate Sorbet, 119
  Sunset Pops, 117
  Wholesome Vanilla Ice Cream, 193
  World's Simplest Soft Serve, The, 131

fruit
  Chewy Strawberry Fruit Leather, 145
  Cinnachips and Rainbow Salsa, 204
  French Toast Kebabs, 33
  Fruit and Nut Snackballs, 148
  Fruity Guac, 168
  fun ways to serve, 35
  Mixed-Berry Fool, 121
  Nutty Fruit Pizza, 122
  See also dried fruit; *specific fruit*
fudge
  Almost-Raw Chocolate Cashew Fudge,
    137
Fudgy Chocolate Frosting, 184

g

garbanzo beans. *See* chickpeas
Garden Wrap-n-Rolls, 58
garfava flour, 64–65, 216–17
GFCF (gluten-free and casein-free) diets,
    xi
Giant Cookie Cake, 189–90
Ginger Chip Drop Cookies, 124–25
Glazed Mini Meat Loaf Muffins, 60–61
gluten and gluten allergies, x, xiii
gluten-free and casein-free (GFCF) diets,
    xi
gluten-free flour mix, 20
Gluten-Free Granola, 12
  Sundaes for Breakfast, 28
gluten-free oats, 12, 215
gluten-free pastas, 215
  See also pasta
Gluten-Free Pie Crust, 139
Gluten-Free Pizza Dough, 48
gluten intolerance, xiii
Gnocchi, Sweet Potato, with Lentils,
    86–88
Golden Gluten-Free Cupcakes, 182

Good-for-You Nachos, 155
granola
  Gluten-Free Granola, 12
  Granola Squares, 152
  Sundaes for Breakfast, 28
gravy
  Farmhouse Buttermilk Biscuits and
    Gravy, 20–22
green beans
  Buffalo Green Beans, 163
  Super Green Pesto Rice Bowl, 76
Green Eggs and Ham Breakfast
    Casserole, 9
Green Monster Dip with Carrot Coins, 194
Greener Sloppy Joes, 91
guacamole
  Fruity Guac, 168

h

ham
  Egg Salad and Ham Sandwich Sticks, 63
  Green Eggs and Ham Breakfast
    Casserole, 9
Healthy Turkey Stir-Fry with Broccoli
    and Cashews, 106
honey, 220
  Almond Flour Honey Cakes, 138
  honey nut tart crust, 134–35
  Soft Pretzels with Honey Mustard
    Sauce, 208–9
hot dogs
  Carnival Corn Dogs, 179
  Franks-n-Beans, 81
hummus
  Zucchini Boats, 162

i

I-Can't-Believe-It's-Not-Buttercream
    Chocolate Cake, 185

ice cream
  Ice Cream Sandwiches for Everyone, 191
  Wholesome Vanilla Ice Cream, 193
Individual Egg-Free Frittatas, 13
Indoors S'mores, 167
ingredients
  labeling, x
  See also pantry items

k

kale
  World's Best Kale Salad, 46
kebabs, 173
  Beef Satay with Peanut Noodles and
    Snow Peas, 98–99
  French Toast Kebabs, 33
  Spicy Mexican Shrimp Skewers, 101
kids, cooking with
  baking sweet potatoes, 27
  crushing nuts, 149
  frosting a cake, 187
  making breaded tofu fingers, 83
  melting chocolate, 126
  rolling out pizza dough, 49
  rolling spring or summer rolls, 181
  shaping a crumb crust, 115
  shaping gnocchi, 88
  zesting and juicing a lime, 52
kiwifruit
  Nutty Fruit Pizza, 122

l

labels, x, 213
lecithin, x
leftovers, 107
lemon
  Easy Lemon Chicken, 103
  Lemony Tuna Salad on Cucumber
    Slices, 70
  Whole-Wheat Lemon Shortbread, 130

lentils, 213
  Garden Wrap-n-Rolls, 58
  Greener Sloppy Joes, 91
  Lentil Burgers, 92
  Sweet Potato Gnocchi with Lentils,
    86–88
lime
  Tahini-Lime Sauce, 43
  zesting and juicing, 52
lunch, 37–72
  Almond Butter-n-Apple 'Wiches, 39
  Barbecue Chicken Salad, 66–67
  Butternut Squash and Zucchini
    Pancakes, 64–65
  Cheddar Avocado Quesadilla, 41
  Corn Chowder with Red Pepper
    Confetti, 45
  Edamame Carrot Falafel Pitas, 43
  Edamame, Carrots, and Shells, 57
  Egg Salad and Ham Sandwich Sticks, 63
  Eggplant, Tomato, and Mozzarella
    Circles, 44
  Garden Wrap-n-Rolls, 58
  Glazed Mini Meat Loaf Muffins, 60–61
  Gluten-Free Pizza Dough, 48
  Lemony Tuna Salad on Cucumber
    Slices, 70
  Mighty Marinara Sauce, 56
  No-Cream of Broccoli Soup, 40
  Pizza Pockets, 47
  Sweet Summer Corn Salad, 50
  tips for packed lunches, 71
  Tomato and Grilled Cheese Soup, 55
  Veggie Bite Soup, 53
  Veggie Sushi Bites, 68
  World's Best Kale Salad, 46

m

Mac-n-Cheeze, 89
malt products, x

mango
  Spicy Mexican Shrimp Skewers, 101
maple syrup, 220
  Crunchy Maple-Walnut Popcorn, 172
  Quinoa Maple Crunch, 14
margarine, 216
Marinara Sauce, Mighty, 56
marshmallows
  Indoors S'mores, 167
meat loaf
  Glazed Mini Meat Loaf Muffins, 60–61
metric conversions and equivalents,
    224–25
Mighty Marinara Sauce, 56
  Chickpea Soldier Dippers for, 30
  Cool Zucchini Noodles, 84
  Corn Chip-Crusted Tofu Fingers with,
    82
  Eggplant, Tomato, and Mozzarella
    Circles, 44
  Pizza Pockets, 47
  Tofu-Stuffed Shells, 75
milk, x
  See also dairy *entries*
milk, nondairy, 221
  Fresh Almond or Rice Milk, 31
  See also coconut and coconut milk
miso paste, 221
Mixed-Berry Fool, 121
molasses, 220
Monkey Bread, Silly, 196–97
mozzarella cheese
  Eggplant, Tomato, and Mozzarella
    Circles, 44
muffins
  Glazed Mini Meat Loaf Muffins, 60–61
  Pumpkin Mini Muffins, 153
  Strawberry Rhubarb Muffins, 16–17
mushrooms
  Buddha Bowls, 80

mushrooms *(continued)*
　Farmhouse Buttermilk Biscuits and
　　Gravy, 20–22
mustard
　Soft Pretzels with Honey Mustard
　　Sauce, 208–9

n

Nachos, Good-for-You, 155
No-Cream of Broccoli Soup, 40
No Moo Chocolate Pudding, 127
noodles
　Beef Satay with Peanut Noodles and
　　Snow Peas, 98–99
　Cool and Crunchy Summer Rolls, 180
　Cool Zucchini Noodles, 84
　See also pasta
nut allergies, xiii–xiv
nutrition, xiv
nutritional yeast, 219
nuts, x, xiii–xiv, 218
　crushing nuts, 149
　honey nut tart crust, 134–35
　nut butters, 218
　See also nut allergies; *specific types*
Nutty Fruit Pizza, 122

o

oat flour, 217
oats, 215
　Carrot Cake Breakfast Cookies, 10
　gluten-free, 12, 215
　Oaty Nut Crumble Sweet Potatoes, 25
　Raspberry Oat Bars, 129
oils, 215–16
olive oil, 215
Olive Oil Twice-Baked Potatoes, 93
1-2-3 Party Mix, 177

onigiri
　Rice Ball Surprise, 160–61
onions
　Caramelized Double-Onion Dip, 211
organic foods, xi, 141
　See also pantry items
oven temperature equivalents, 225

p

pancakes
　Blueberry Corncakes, 6
　Butternut Squash and Zucchini
　　Pancakes, 64–65
pantry items, 213–21
　beans, grains, and pastas, 213–15
　fats, 215–16
　flours and starches, 216–17
　fruits, nuts, and seeds, 218
　miscellaneous items, 221
　spices, vinegars, and flavorings, 218–19
　sweeteners, 220
paprika, 219
parsnips
　oven fries, 173
　Veggie Bite Soup, 53
parties, 175–212
　activities, 212
　Animal Bagels, 178
　Black Bean Brownie Bites, 205
　Caramelized Double-Onion Dip, 211
　Carnival Corn Dogs, 179
　Cinnachips and Rainbow Salsa, 204
　Cool and Crunchy Summer Rolls, 180
　Crispy Cheese Bites with Bean Salsa,
　　210
　Dairy-Free Vanilla Frosting, 186
　Double Chocolate Chunk Cookies, 192
　Fudgy Chocolate Frosting, 184
　Giant Cookie Cake, 189–90

Golden Gluten-Free Cupcakes, 182
Green Monster Dip with Carrot Coins,
　194
I-Can't-Believe-It's-Not-Buttercream
　Chocolate Cake, 185
Ice Cream Sandwiches for Everyone, 191
1-2-3 Party Mix, 177
Party-On Chili, 198
Polenta Mini Pizzas, 201
Silly Monkey Bread, 196–97
Soft Pretzels with Honey Mustard
　Sauce, 208–9
South of the Border Sushi, 202
Sunny Candy Pops, 203
Sweet and Salty Popcorn Balls, 199
Teriyaki Turkey Sliders, 206
Wholesome Vanilla Ice Cream, 193
party mix
　1-2-3 Party Mix, 177
pasta
　Edamame, Carrots, and Shells, 57
　Mac-n-Cheeze, 89
　Mighty Marinara Sauce, 56
　pasta frittata, 107
　Sweet Potato Gnocchi with Lentils,
　　86–88
　Tofu-Stuffed Shells, 75
　See also noodles
peaches
　Autumn Buckwheat and Flax Porridge,
　　15
　barbecue sauce, 66
　Raw Summer Peach Tart, 134–35
　strawberry-peach muffins, 17
peanut allergies, xiii–xiv
peanuts and peanut butter, x
　Beef Satay with Peanut Noodles and
　　Snow Peas, 98–99
　Indoors S'mores, 167

pears
  Pear Dunkers with Cashew-Cinnamon
    Yogurt Sauce, 146
  Saucy Pears and Butternut Squash,
    170–71
peas
  Beef Satay with Peanut Noodles and
    Snow Peas, 98–99
  Chicken Potpie with Sweet Potato
    Topping, 94–96
  Tuna-Brown Rice Bake, 97
  Veggie Bite Soup, 53
pecans
  Black Bean Brownie Bites, 205
  honey nut tart crust, 134–35
peppers. *See* bell peppers
pesto
  Super Green Pesto Rice Bowl, 76
pie
  Chocolate Crumb Crust, 114
  Coconut No-Cream Pie, 113
  Gluten-Free Pie Crust, 139
  shaping a crumb crust, 115
  Spiced Pumpkin Pie, 140
pineapple
  barbecue sauce, 66
  Sunset Pops, 117
pitas
  Edamame Carrot Falafel Pitas, 43
pizza
  Cheesy Stuffed Pizza Burgers, 102
  Nutty Fruit Pizza, 122
  Pizza Pockets, 47
  Polenta Mini Pizzas, 201
pizza dough
  Gluten-Free Pizza Dough, 48
  rolling out, 49
  veggie pockets, 107
plum vinegar, 219
Polenta Mini Pizzas, 201

popcorn
  Crunchy Maple-Walnut Popcorn, 172
  1-2-3 Party Mix, 177
  Sweet and Salty Popcorn Balls, 199
popsicles
  Sunset Pops, 117
pork
  All-Day Roast Pork Shoulder, 104–5
  Glazed Mini Meat Loaf Muffins, 60–61
Porridge, Autumn Buckwheat and Flax, 15
potato flour, 217
potato starch, 217
potatoes
  Easy Lemon Chicken, 103
  hot potato dance, 212
  No-Cream of Broccoli Soup, 40
  Olive Oil Twice-Baked Potatoes, 93
  potato-stuffed peppers, 107
Potpie, Chicken, with Sweet Potato
  Topping, 94–96
pretzels
  Soft Pretzels with Honey Mustard
    Sauce, 208–9
  Sweet and Salty Popcorn Balls, 199
pudding
  Brown Rice Breakfast Pudding, 8
  No Moo Chocolate Pudding, 127
pumpkin
  Pumpkin Mini Muffins, 153
  Spiced Pumpkin Pie, 140
pumpkin seeds, 218
  Carrot Cake Breakfast Cookies, 10
  Granola, 12
  1-2-3 Party Mix, 177

q

Quesadilla, Cheddar Avocado, 41
quinoa, 215
  Buddha Bowls, 80

Quinoa Maple Crunch, 14
  rinsing, 53
  Veggie Bite Soup, 53

r

Rainbow Salsa, Cinnachips and, 204
raspberries, raspberry jam
  Raspberry Oat Bars, 129
  Sundaes for Breakfast, 28
  Sunset Pops, 117
raw cane sugar, 220
Raw Summer Peach Tart, 134–35
red peppers. *See* bell peppers
rhubarb
  Strawberry Rhubarb Muffins, 16–17
rice, 215
  Buddha Bowls, 80
  Rice Ball Surprise, 160–61
  Super Green Pesto Rice Bowl, 76
  Tuna-Brown Rice Bake, 97
rice flour, 217
rice milk, 221
  Fresh Rice Milk, 31
rice wine vinegar, 219
rosemary
  Chickpea Herb Crackers, 151

s

salads
  Barbecue Chicken Salad, 66–67
  Lemony Tuna Salad on Cucumber
    Slices, 70
  Sweet Summer Corn Salad, 50
  World's Best Kale Salad, 46
salsa
  Cinnachips and Rainbow Salsa, 204
  Crispy Cheese Bites with Bean Salsa,
    210
Salted Caramel Hot Cocoa, 132

sandwiches
  Almond Butter-n-Apple 'Wiches, 39
  Chocolate Toasties, 111
  Egg Salad and Ham Sandwich Sticks, 63
  Greener Sloppy Joes, 91
  Pizza Pockets, 47
  Tomato and Grilled Cheese Soup, 55
  veggie pockets, 107
  See also burgers; pitas
Satay, Beef, with Peanut Noodles and
  Snow Peas, 98–99
sauces
  barbecue sauce, 66
  Mighty Marinara Sauce, 56
  peanut sauce, 98–99
  Soft Pretzels with Honey Mustard
    Sauce, 208–9
  summer roll dipping sauce, 180
  Tahini-Lime Sauce, 43
  See also dips; salsa
Saucy Pears and Butternut Squash,
  170–71
Savory Roasted Chickpeas, 156
seitan, x
sesame oil, 216
sesame seeds, 218
  Edamame, Carrots, and Shells, 57
  Yogurt-Sesame Sweet Potatoes, 24
shellfish and shellfish allergies, x, xiii
  See also shrimp
Shortbread, Whole-Wheat Lemon, 130
shrimp
  Spicy Mexican Shrimp Skewers, 101
Silly Monkey Bread, 196–97
Sliders, Teriyaki Turkey, 206
Sloppy Joes, Greener, 91
smoked paprika, 219
S'mores, Indoors, 167
snacks, 143–73
  Apple Sun Smiles, 166

Buffalo Green Beans, 163
Chewy Strawberry Fruit Leather, 145
Chickpea Herb Crackers, 151
Chocolate Cinnamon Crisps, 165
Crunchy Maple-Walnut Popcorn, 172
Fruit and Nut Snackballs, 148
Fruity Guac, 168
Good-for-You Nachos, 155
Granola Squares, 152
ideas for, 173
Indoors S'mores, 167
Pear Dunkers with Cashew-Cinnamon
  Yogurt Sauce, 146
Pumpkin Mini Muffins, 153
Rice Ball Surprise, 160–61
Saucy Pears and Butternut Squash,
  170–71
Savory Roasted Chickpeas, 156
Spiced Carrot Fries, 158
Sunset Pops, 117
Walnut-Stuffed Figs, 157
Zucchini Boats, 162
See also cookies; parties
Snow Peas, Beef Satay with Peanut
  Noodles and, 98–99
Soft Pretzels with Honey Mustard Sauce,
  208–9
Sorbet, Cherry Chocolate, 119
sorghum flour, 217
soups
  Corn Chowder with Red Pepper
    Confetti, 45
  No-Cream of Broccoli Soup, 40
  Party-On Chili, 198
  Veggie Bite Soup, 53
  white chicken chili, 107
South of the Border Sushi, 202
Southwest Beans and Corn Bread Bake,
  78–79
soy and soy allergies, x, xiii

soy foods. *See* edamame; tofu
Spiced Carrot Fries, 158
Spiced Pumpkin Pie, 140
spices, 218–19
Spicy Mexican Shrimp Skewers, 101
spinach
  Barbecue Chicken Salad, 66–67
  Green Eggs and Ham Breakfast
    Casserole, 9
  Green Monster Dip with Carrot Coins,
    194
  Individual Egg-Free Frittatas, 13
  Tofu Scramble with Spinach, 19
squash
  Glazed Mini Meat Loaf Muffins, 60–61
  oven fries, 173
  See also butternut squash; pumpkin;
    zucchini
starches, 217
Stir-fry, Healthy Turkey, with Broccoli
  and Cashews, 106
strawberries
  Chewy Strawberry Fruit Leather, 145
  Chocolate Cinnamon Crisps with, 165
  Strawberry Rhubarb Muffins, 16–17
substitutions
  applesauce in baked goods, 221
  for buttermilk, 219
  for eggs, 216–218
  for sugar, 220
sugar, 109, 141, 220
  alternatives to, 220
Summer Rolls, Cool and Crunchy, 180
Sundaes for Breakfast, 28
sunflower seeds or butter, 218
  Apple Sun Smiles, 166
  Chocolate Toasties, 111
  Cool Zucchini Noodles, 84
  Granola Squares, 152
  Indoors S'mores, 167

sunflower seed granola, 12

Sunny Candy Pops, 203

Sunny Candy Pops, 203

Sunset Pops, 117

Super Green Pesto Rice Bowl, 76

Super Sweet Potatoes, 23

sushi

Rice Ball Surprise, 160–61

South of the Border Sushi, 202

Veggie Sushi Bites, 68

Sweet and Salty Popcorn Balls, 199

sweet potatoes

baking with kids, 27

Chicken Potpie with Sweet Potato
Topping, 94–96

Frankenstein Sweet Potatoes, 26

Oaty Nut Crumble Sweet Potatoes, 25

oven fries, 173

Super Sweet Potatoes, 23

Sweet Potato Gnocchi with Lentils,
86–88

Yogurt-Sesame Sweet Potatoes, 24

Sweet Summer Corn Salad, 50

Swiss chard

Barbecue Chicken Salad, 66–67

Super Green Pesto Rice Bowl, 76

t

Tacos, Breakfast On-the-Go, 7

tahini, 218

Banana Chocolate Shakeroo, 34

Green Monster Dip with Carrot Coins,
194

Individual Egg-Free Frittatas, 13

Tahini-Lime Sauce, 43

Wholesome Vanilla Ice Cream, 193

World's Best Kale Salad, 46

Zucchini Boats, 162

tamari, 219

tapioca starch, 217

Tart, Raw Summer Peach, 134–35

Teriyaki Turkey Sliders, 206

tofu, 221

Animal Bagels, 178

Buddha Bowls, 80

Coconut No-Cream Pie, 113

Corn Chip-Crusted Tofu Fingers, 82

French Toast Kebabs, 33

Individual Egg-Free Frittatas, 13

No Moo Chocolate Pudding, 127

Spiced Pumpkin Pie, 140

Tofu Scramble with Spinach, 19

Tofu-Stuffed Shells, 75

tomato sauce

Greener Sloppy Joes, 91

Mighty Marinara Sauce, 56

Polenta Mini Pizzas, 201

Tofu-Stuffed Shells, 75

Veggie Bite Soup, 53

tomatoes

Barbecue Chicken Salad, 66–67

barbecue sauce, 66

Eggplant, Tomato, and Mozzarella
Circles, 44

South of the Border Sushi, 202

Sweet Summer Corn Salad, 50

Tomato and Grilled Cheese Soup, 55

tortilla chips

Corn Chip-Crusted Tofu Fingers, 82

Good-for-You Nachos, 155

tortillas

Cheddar Avocado Quesadilla, 41

Chocolate Cinnamon Crisps, 165

Cinnachips and Rainbow Salsa, 204

South of the Border Sushi, 202

See also tacos

trans fats, 216

tree nuts. *See* nuts; *specific types*

tuna
  Lemony Tuna Salad on Cucumber
    Slices, 70
  Rice Ball Surprise, 160–61
  Tuna-Brown Rice Bake, 97
turkey, ground
  Cheesy Stuffed Pizza Burgers, 102
  Healthy Turkey Stir-Fry with Broccoli
    and Cashews, 106
  Teriyaki Turkey Sliders, 206
turmeric, 219

u

umeboshi plum vinegar, 219

v

vanilla
  Dairy-Free Vanilla Frosting, 186
  Wholesome Vanilla Ice Cream, 193
vegetable shortening, 216
vegetables
  Animal Bagels, 178
  oven fries, 158, 173
  snack ideas, 173
  Veggie Bite Soup, 53
  veggie pockets, 107
  Veggie Sushi Bites, 68
  See also specific vegetables
vinegars, 219

w

waffles
  Banana Bread Waffles, 5
  Green Eggs and Ham Breakfast
    Casserole, 9
walnuts
  Crunchy Maple-Walnut Popcorn, 172

walnut and fig granola, 12
Walnut-Stuffed Figs, 157
wheat, x, xiii
  whole-wheat flours, 216
  Whole-Wheat Lemon Shortbread, 130
  whole-wheat pasta, 215
  See also gluten entries
wheat allergies, xiii
white chicken chili, 107
Wholesome Vanilla Ice Cream, 193
  Ice Cream Sandwiches for Everyone, 191
World's Best Kale Salad, 46
World's Simplest Soft Serve, The, 131

x

xanthan gum, 217

y

yellow miso paste, 221
yogurt
  Pear Dunkers with Cashew-Cinnamon
    Yogurt Sauce, 146
  Sundaes for Breakfast, 28
  Yogurt-Sesame Sweet Potatoes, 24

z

zucchini
  Butternut Squash and Zucchini
    Pancakes, 64–65
  Cool Zucchini Noodles, 84
  Healthy Turkey Stir-Fry with Broccoli
    and Cashews, 106
  Lentil Burgers, 92
  Southwest Beans and Corn Bread Bake,
    78–79
  Zucchini Boats, 162

NAME

ADDRESS

CITY/STATE/ZIP

EMAIL ADDRESS (REQUIRED)

Limit one subscription per book purchase.

The order must be accompanied by the original redemption form page from the cookbook. No photocopies, scans or duplication of any kind will be accepted. Offer open to U.S. residents only. If you're already a subscriber, your subscription will be extended. Your first issue mails within 6 to 8 weeks of receipt. We will notify you via email when we've received your redemption form.